DAY-VOTIONS™

DAY-VOTIONS™
for women

Heart to Heart
Encouragement

Rebecca Barlow Jordan

ZONDERVAN®

ZONDERVAN.com/
AUTHORTRACKER
follow your favorite authors

We want to hear from you. Please send your comments about this book to us in care of zreview@zondervan.com. Thank you.

ZONDERVAN

Day-votions™ for Women
Copyright © 2009 by Rebecca Barlow Jordan

This title is also available as a Zondervan ebook.
Visit www.zondervan.com/ebooks.

This title is also available in a Zondervan audio edition.
Visit www.zondervan.fm.

Requests for information should be addressed to:

Zondervan, *Grand Rapids, Michigan 49530*

Library of Congress Cataloging-in-Publication Data

Jordan, Rebecca.
    Day-votions for women : heart-to-heart encouragement /
Rebecca Barlow Jordan.
       p. cm.
    Includes bibliographical references.
    ISBN 978-0-310-32203-0 (hardcover, jacketed)
    1. Christian women — Prayers and devotions I. Title.
BV4844.J68 — 2009
242'.643 — dc22
                                          2009040174

Interior design: Michelle Espinoza

Printed in the United States of America

---

10 11 12 13 14 15 /DCI/ 20 19 18 17 16 15 14 13 12 11 10 9 8 7 6 5 4 3 2 1

To every woman who longs to strengthen
her relationship with God and others

contents

special thanks

In writing a book of encouragement for others, I must thank those who have encouraged me in the process. So many have had a part.

I'm so thankful for a great editor like Sue Brower, who has been like a cheerleader — patiently encouraging, listening, answering questions, and believing in my writing. Her enthusiasm about this project from day one has filled me with an even greater passion to write my heart. You're the best, Sue! Thanks also to freelance editor Lori VandenBosch for her editing and encouraging comments, and to Verlyn Verbrugge for his editing skills. Thanks to marketing director Karwyn Bursma and her extremely talented team for their beautiful work on the book's cover and creativity in their marketing.

I appreciate Joyce Ondersma and Jackie Aldridge in author relations and the wonderful Zondervan sales team. And to the entire Zondervan staff, including support team, for your willingness to publish this project. How can I say thank you enough for all you do? This book would not be possible without all of you at Zondervan.

A special thanks to Steve Laube, for his integrity and diligence as my agent and friend. His invaluable background and knowledge of the writing business have given superb direction to my writing. I so appreciate his encouragement and patience, his belief in my gifts, and his ability to find a home for my writing dreams so quickly. Thank you, Steve, for your enthusiasm for this new Day-votions series.

Thanks to my friend Karen-Atkins Milton, who gave generously of her time to look over many of these day-votions and offer another woman's perspective. To those who prayed for me throughout the writing of this book: my precious daughters and sons-in-law, Valerie, Jennifer, Shawn, and Craig; other family members, friends, church members, my Bible study class, and the women of my personal prayer support team: Priscilla Adams, Mary Griffin, Ruth Inman, Sharon Hogan, and Kim Coffman — your prayers and encouragement made such a difference. Thanks also to those friends who shared transparent examples from their lives in the book that will no doubt encourage many in their walk with the Lord.

There is no way to adequately thank my precious husband for his prayers, support, and encouragement. Larry not only blessed me by offering his thorough editing skills and great communication abilities in reading through every day-votion. He gave up his own comfort and rare personal time, taking over many of my everyday tasks to do whatever was necessary to help me complete this manuscript. With his love, integrity, and unselfishness he has influenced this writing more than anyone else, so that together, we could be a team in ministry. I could not write without his loving support. I love you, Larry! You are one of God's greatest blessings to me!

And to my precious heavenly Father and Lord Jesus, there will never be enough words to adequately praise you for who you are. Nor could I ever count the times you have continually blessed me in ways I could never deserve. For every time I cry "I can't!" you always answer, "But I can." You, Lord, are the passion of my heart. You are the One who encourages me daily, who satisfies my soul hunger, and who fills me with purpose. Thank you for allowing me the joy of writing about you and the privilege of sharing encouragement with others.

encouragement for women

Professionals may not agree as to what women really need in life. Even we, as women, don't always know ourselves. Overstressed and in need of rest, we search for quiet places to restore and regroup. Yet feeling isolated and alone, we crave understanding and companionship — others who will share our load and celebrate our joys.

We are not all alike. God created us as unique individuals. And yet we are the same. Every woman needs — and wants — encouragement and deeper, more meaningful relationships.

For years I've tried to write devotions that would encourage readers to connect on a deeper level with God and others: to "love the Lord your God with all your heart and with all your soul and with all your strength and with all your mind," and to "love your neighbor as yourself" (Luke 10:27). But sometimes "life" happens, and we women forget how to do that. We realize that love hurts and relationships take work. Energy gets zapped, hearts are broken, and our minds get confused. We forget what we were made for, and we forget how much God truly loves us. Yet the longing for connection lingers, like the fragrance in a home when a sweet candle's flame has been extinguished.

I could offer you a few motivational thoughts to lift your spirits temporarily, but they would not satisfy your heart hunger for long. In this new series of Day-votions™, I've tried to say to you as women, "You are not alone." None of us are. Our very existence depends on strong relationships. In bite-sized, *day-votions* for everyday living, I've written some nuggets of spiritual encouragement that I hope will help you strengthen your relationship with God and others. I pray these stories, insights, and biblical truths will direct you to the only One who can meet all of your needs. As you draw close to Jesus, I believe he will connect the dots to more meaningful relationships with others as well.

Whether you're dealing with finances, inadequacy, loneliness, or guilt, you're not alone in your struggle. Other women have — and are — walking the same path as you. It doesn't matter if you're single, married, young, middle-aged, or a senior, God is by your side, applauding your work, extending fresh hope, and drawing you close to himself so he can whisper, "You *are* making a difference. I'm here to help you, and I will take care of you. I love you. I always will."

Through these pages, I hope you'll laugh a little and maybe cry a little; but more than anything, my heart's desire is that you will be encouraged to keep on loving, laughing, serving, and sharing — and that you will gain a new sense of joy and purpose in this beautiful, God-ordained role of being a woman.

"May our Lord Jesus himself and God our Father, who loved us and by his grace gave us eternal encouragement and good hope, encourage your hearts and strengthen you in every good deed and word" (2 Thessalonians 2:16 – 17).

Rebecca

A woman who knows
she is deeply loved,
completely forgiven,
totally accepted,
and inwardly treasured by Christ
will most likely teach others
the same truths.

— RBJ

day 1
the perfect storm

He got up and rebuked the wind and the raging waters;
the storm subsided, and all was calm.
Luke 8:24

It wasn't exactly a *bad* day. *Challenging,* definitely.

The apricot and white tabby looked so cute on my back doorstep curled up in a ball. I had seen it slinking under the gate and into my backyard several times, but I usually ignored it. *Maybe it will catch our newly discovered mice,* I thought. I had no idea who owned the cat, if anyone. It had no tags, only a flea collar.

I stepped outside and leaned down to pet the cat. At first it purred softly as if to say, *"More, More!"* Then suddenly the cat lunged, sinking its needle-sharp teeth into my right hand. I yelped and ran inside.

It was 7:30 a.m. and we were unable to locate the owner. So I called Animal Control. They called back when they opened, suggesting I call my doctor. Later I talked to a neighbor who thought she knew the cat's owners, who were at work.

I couldn't get a doctor's appointment until later that afternoon. His office was an hour away. "You need a tetanus shot and possibly antibiotics," said the nurse.

Later she called back. "We have no vaccine. Do you still want to come in?" I knew I probably needed antibiotics, because my hand was already swollen with red streaks. I secured the appointment but spent the next two hours playing phone tag trying to find a place where I could get a tetanus shot. In order to save time, I finally tried a community health clinic in another town on the way to my doctor.

Before I left town, I needed to trade cars with my husband at his workplace. Exhausted by the ordeal already, I began quietly quoting, "You will keep in perfect peace those whose minds are steadfast, because they trust in you" (Isaiah 26:3). But perfect peace doesn't always mean perfect circumstances. Sometimes it includes the perfect storm.

> *Perfect peace doesn't always mean perfect circumstances.*
> *Sometimes it includes the perfect storm.*

I traded cars, but backed straight into another parked car in my path. By this time I was shaking as I found my husband and reported the bad news. The other car wasn't even scratched, but the impact cracked our bumper across the middle. Larry just held me. "It will be all right. Don't worry about it."

Thirty minutes later I arrived at the clinic for my tetanus shot and saw a room full of waiting patients, coughing children and adults. It was flu season.

An hour and a half later I walked into the doors of my doctor's office building. The revolving doors stuck — shut down completely — with me in it. I pushed hard, finally opening it. When I reached the doctor's office upstairs, I realized my doctor had moved. So I retreated and drove to what I thought was his new location. Wrong place. Fortunately, I had the office number on my cell phone, so I called to get directions.

Later in his office my doctor took one look at my wound and promptly prescribed antibiotics. He knew we were leaving town in five days, so he cautioned me about keeping in touch with Animal Control and the ten-day window for rabies treatment. "You need to find the cat and have it quarantined." *No*, I thought. *Probably not a good idea for* me *to find the cat.*

It was late afternoon by the time I returned home. I figured we were safe by now. After all, the day was winding down. Surely Animal Control had quarantined the cat by now. Wrong. As I drove into my driveway, my cell phone rang.

"Mrs. Jordan? It's Animal Control. We've been driving around your neighborhood all day, but we haven't found the cat." About that time, the cat strolled by, not twenty yards away.

"Come now!" I yelled. "Here's the cat!"

After he arrived, we both tried — and failed — to coax the cat into the waiting truck. Still no sign of the owners. I finally left to get my prescription. Waiting time? An hour. So I bought groceries. My hand was puffy, bleeding, and throbbing. An hour and a half later I pulled into my driveway with my expensive supply of antibiotics and trunk full of groceries. As I shut the trunk, the car alarm sounded, "Beep! Beep! Beep! Beep!" announcing my arrival to the neighbors. I ran into the house, scrounging for my keys to shut off the noise.

A few minutes later, my husband walked in the door with a bouquet of roses and took me in his arms. "These are for you. I know you've had a bad day. By the way, they quarantined the cat."

And in that moment, all the frustrations and "challenges" of the day melted away as I fell into my husband's embrace, weeping. To me, he was a picture of God "with skin on."

Sometimes as a woman, you may feel like storm clouds hover over you day in and day out. Whether accompanied by angry winds or persistent rain, at the end of your "perfect storm," you may or may not have someone with skin on to greet you and wipe away your tears. But at the end of every day, there is One who *will* be standing there, arms open wide, whispering, "I'm here. I care. And I love you." Sweeter than the most fragrant bouquet is Jesus, the Rose of Sharon.

And when that happens, suddenly your "bad, challenging day" is but a distant memory as you bask in the sheer joy of his comforting embrace.

DAY-BREAK

Describe one of your most challenging days. How did you handle it? If it happened again, what would you do differently, if anything? What did God teach you through that experience?

DAY-BRIEF

Purr-fect days only exist in the movies.

DAY-VOTEDLY YOURS

Jesus, what would I do without you? Where would I turn if you were not there? Thank you for giving me strength when I feel none of my own. Thank you for holding me when I feel like falling apart.

day 2
the silent majority

Leave her alone ... She did what she could.
Mark 14:6, 8

A silver-gray casket sat in the center of the funeral home chapel. A huge mound of pink and white carnations adorned the top.

Friends and family, mourners of the deceased woman, packed the chapel. This woman had accomplished no great tasks. Few knew her beyond the city limits where she had lived most of her life. No books contained her life story. No streets carried her name. No history lessons would include her deeds. But I suspected heaven's books boasted of numerous notations about this one-talent, simple woman.

The pastor's eulogy was simple and short. At the end of the service he summed up her life in one sentence: "Like the woman who poured expensive perfume on Jesus' head, this woman, too, did what she could."

I thought about those words. In today's culture, we celebrate "famous" women for their ravishing beauty, their educational accomplishments, and their record-breaking success. Doing what we *can* is considered too average. Haven't you at one time or another struggled with the thought of, *I should do more, be more. What is my life counting for?* We compare ourselves with other noteworthy candidates and mutter, "*Am I doing enough? I can never do enough.*"

Others applaud women when they overcome challenges, whether in position, prestige, or influential power. No one can deny the powerful influence of a woman, even in biblical times: Esther, an orphaned Jewish girl crowned queen of a Persian empire, and chosen to save her people from annihilation; Deborah, a judge and leader who took office because no man would accept the challenge; Mary, a godly, devoted young woman who, by the miraculous power of God's Spirit, gave birth to Jesus, the Son of God. And there are so many more throughout the years who each fulfilled a dramatic role in God's plan that helped shape — and change — the world.

> *The worth of a woman has everything to do with being God's child and fulfilling our purpose in his plan, whatever he assigns.*

But both Scripture and history reveal the silent majority — hundreds and thousands of women like you and me — mothers, singles, grandmothers, women of all races and places in life — who will never be known this side of heaven except to a few friends and family.

The worth of a woman is often so grossly misunderstood. Her value has nothing to do with beauty or brains or success. It has everything to do with being God's child and fulfilling our purpose in his plan, whatever he assigns.

Those like the woman who poured out all her love and costly extravagance on the head of Jesus near the end of his life, and this woman whose friends and family poured out their praises and blessings at the end of hers — these did what they could. And it was enough.

Whatever you bring to God's feet, however your life honors him, wherever he places your life and influence — do what you can. And it will be enough for you too.

DAY-BREAK

Who are the people God has placed in your life? List some of the ways they have influenced you. Take time to thank them this week. In one sentence, how would you like someone to summarize your life?

DAY-BRIEF

When you do what you can with love, it will always be enough.

DAY-VOTEDLY YOURS

Lord Jesus, whatever I have to give, whether small or great, is yours. Use me, my gifts, my life, my all for your glory. My greatest desire is to simply fulfill your purpose for my life.

day 3
throwing on the towel

Now that I, your Lord and Teacher, have washed your feet,
you also should wash one another's feet. I have set you
an example that you should do as I have done for you.
John 13:14 – 15

Nancy (not her real name) plopped down on the living room couch, exhausted. She had just returned from a family Thanksgiving celebration filled with emotional challenges. She laughed out loud. Family. Who redefined that word, anyway? Her husband or her sister?

A year ago, Nancy's husband had announced he wanted a divorce. One month later, he married another woman. Not just any woman. He married her sister! The sting of rejection and betrayal shook Nancy's world, and her life was ripping apart. How would she respond? How *should* she respond?

Life, no matter how fulfilling, includes unexpected challenges: earth-shaking events, emotional upheavals, personal attacks, or even unfulfilled dreams. It can happen to us or to those we love. Our first response may be to clench our fists and grind our teeth. *How could this happen to me? What makes Christians act so ugly? Where is God in all this?*

Nancy dealt with her anger positively and refused to retaliate. At times she felt like giving up, yet she pleaded for God's help. Only months after the divorce, she invited her former husband and her sister to a "family" get-together. Her continual attempts to do the right thing so affected her husband that he knew — and admitted his mistake soon after. Nancy still suffered the loss of a broken marriage, but she demonstrated something precious by her godly response.

When life got tough, Jesus turned to towel washing.

Tiring and unfair circumstances may tempt us as women to throw in the towel, but God designed another solution. Jesus spent almost three years teaching his band of disciples. Trying to harness the potential of twelve unruly misfits could have caused anyone to surrender, but not Jesus. When life got tough, he turned to towel washing — even the very feet of the one Jesus *knew* would soon betray him, Judas Iscariot. Humbling himself, Jesus chose to live by faithful example, showing his disciples the full extent of his love. Instead of throwing *in* the towel, he threw *on* the towel.

The example he left those twelve disciples lingers on in the writings and practice of his followers. The path to deeper intimacy with God is not easy. Some relationships will try our patience and tempt us to react, rather than respond. But God wants to help us do what is right.

And what is right? Anything Jesus did — including "throwing on the towel."

DAY-BREAK

When are you most tempted to "throw in the towel"? Plan now how you'll respond to your next trying circumstance — or relationship. What can you do to "throw on the towel" instead?

DAY-BRIEF

Wise women wear a big smile — and carry a big towel.

DAY-VOTEDLY YOURS

Jesus, you suffered injustice, rejection, sorrow, and pain at the hands of angry people. Yet you never complained, and you never sought revenge. Make me more like you, Jesus! I have a long way to go.

day 4
didn't i tell you?

"Lord," Martha said to Jesus, "if you had been here,
my brother would not have died. But I know that even now
God will give you whatever you ask."
Jesus said to her, "Your brother will rise again."
Martha answered, "I know he will rise again
in the resurrection at the last day."
John 11:21 – 24

The familiar words of a commercial ring out: "I want it all ... I want it NOW!"

None of us likes delays.

When God has other plans from what we've written on our to-do list, we don't always understand. Isn't he a God of order? Doesn't he care about our needs? Aren't we supposed to make plans? Doesn't what I want matter?

If our desires involve selfishness, like the jingle above, hopefully we can figure that out. God may be trying to correct our hearts. But what about when God has given us assurance that a certain answer is coming, like Jesus' promise to Mary and Martha that he would heal Lazarus? Jesus delays, and we see nothing happening, or we experience the opposite of what we thought God promised. That's a harder scenario.

We desperately cry for a reason: "Why the delay?" And too

often, we may hear only … silence. But God has a plan. If we will wait and not waver, God will reveal it to us, step by step, day by day. In the meantime, we know that regardless of the outcome, when God is in control, every delay will be "for God's glory," as Jesus said about Lazarus's sickness (John 11:4). We *know* that in our heads, but our hearts don't always agree.

As women we may wonder, *What about in the meantime? How can we set our clocks to God's time?* God understood Mary and Martha's hearts. He allowed them to speak their feelings of disappointment, and even their misunderstanding. His tenderness and compassion shone through his words and empathetic tears when Jesus finally showed up after Lazarus had already died: "Jesus wept" (John 11:35).

In our objections and confusion, Jesus states again to us, as he did to Martha: "Did I not tell you that if you believe, you will see the glory of God?" (John 11:40).

> ### When God is in control, every delay will be "for God's glory."

How can we handle our confusion? We can do what Martha did, even though she didn't understand. We don't keep focusing on the unknown. Instead we rehearse what we do know about Jesus. We search our hearts for familiar truths. We search his Word for personal promises. Then we wait … with a different kind of expectation.

Go ahead. Try it. Close your eyes and imagine Jesus standing in front of you, holding your hand, looking you in the eye, and gently but firmly speaking those same words: "My child, didn't I tell you, that if you believed, you'd see?" And we remove the stone of unbelief to find his words are true.

What if the delay didn't result in the answer you expected or hoped for? Somehow, it doesn't matter anymore. Because in rehearsing what you did know, you discovered the words "for God's glory" are not at all about what you want or when you want it. In fact, the meaning of those words may stretch into the unknown. You may never understand this side of heaven.

But it's okay.

DAY-BREAK

List all the things you do know about God — his names, his character, his attributes. What do you know about Jesus personally? Look for Bible verses that begin "I know ..." or promises that define what we can know about him. Then "rehearse" those truths and promises daily.

DAY-BRIEF

Knowledge is power, when used rightly.

DAY-VOTEDLY YOURS

Jesus, I know that you are my Redeemer, faithful and true; I know that you love me with an unconditional love. I know that you created me, that I am always on your mind daily, that you died for me, and that you are the resurrection and the life. And I know that even in your delays, you have more than my own interests at heart. Most of all, you have God's glory in mind.

day 5

staying power

The man who had been demon-possessed begged to go with him. Jesus
did not let him, but said, "Go home to your family
and tell them how much the Lord has done for you,
and how he has had mercy on you."
Mark 5:18 – 19 NIV

I hear from women often who long to make a difference for Christ. Some even admit their envy of those whom God seems to use in greater ways. Some, like this demon-possessed man, feel God has done a great work in their lives, and they immediately envision a new or expanded "ministry," fields ready for harvest — and they, as the gatherers of God's fruit. They want to follow Jesus and his power wherever he goes. They want *more*.

But "ministry" doesn't always mean new or greater fields. We are willing to go where there's greater action, but what if God says, "Stay with your family"?

God reserves the right to dispense the right resources and pick the places where he wants us to serve him. On the one hand, as long as we are seeking to please him and bring glory to God, anywhere is the right place to serve. On the other hand, God designs special opportunities and tasks only he can make known. Running ahead of him only brings frustration and disappointment.

Perhaps the hardest place for us as women to witness and minister for Jesus is within the walls of our own home, city, or workplace. Others who never knew us elsewhere may see a life on fire, but they cannot identify the before and after like the ones already in our communities. At home, people *know* you. Friends and acquaintances may think, *How long will they last? What difference will all this make next week, next month, or next year? Is this really a work of God?*

If God says to you, "Stay where you are," he doesn't mean for you to hide your testimony from others or deny the amazing work God has done in your life. The greatest challenge we women face is in the daily places where we rub shoulders with the people in our family and in our community. And the greatest test of God's power and reality in our lives is learning how to depend on God right where we are.

> *The greatest test of God's power in our lives is learning how to depend on God right where we are.*

God may call you to "greater fields." And if he does, rest assured his power will go with you if you constantly depend on his presence to guide you. He knows what inevitably will bring his heart — and yours — more joy. If you truly want "more" of *him*, and not just more miracles or greater ministries, God will open up opportunities far greater than you can ever ask for, hope, or imagine.

But God also transfers his power to the trenches. To those who believe, trust, and obey, God may say, "Go home and tell."

He will do the rest.

DAY-BREAK

What are your greatest challenges in your place of service? Why do you think God has placed you where you are? Do you ever long for greater fields of ministry?

DAY-BRIEF

The question is not, "Will God show up?" But will we?

DAY-VOTEDLY YOURS

Lord, my heart's desire is to honor you wherever I go. If that means greater fields, I'm open to that. But if not, show me how to make your name known in even greater ways where I am.

day 6
she has it all

Who can find a virtuous woman? For her price is far above rubies.
Proverbs 31:10 KJV

If you've ever studied Proverbs 31 or heard of "The Proverbs Woman," you may have thought, *Who could possibly be that woman?*

I admit I've often wondered the same thing. My answer to that question of "Who can find a virtuous woman?" would have to be, "I don't know, but it's not me." Trying to mimic her in my younger years left me feeling like an athlete who had just run a marathon in the Olympics — only to cross the finish line in last place.

Just look at her exhaustive character traits: a woman of strength, honor, initiative, kindness, generosity, organization, trustworthiness, wisdom, dignity, talent, inner beauty. No wonder this woman is worth far more than rubies! Is there such a woman?

To her children, she's a supermom; to her husband, his crown and glory. To her neighbors, she's an angel; to her community, she's a godsend. But to the average twenty-first-century woman, this wonder woman may represent an impossible ideal — a figment of some wishful mother-in-law's imagination! Take a closer look. If you are a mother, what kind of daughters do you want to raise? What kind of wives do you want your sons to marry? What kind of woman do you want to be? Don't the qualities of this ideal woman characterize Christ himself?

Most likely, we won't find a woman with all of her qualifications. Wool-spinning, carefully planted vineyards, royal tapestries, hand-sewn clothing, thoroughly organized households, volunteer work for the needy, and flourishing business ventures — all simultaneous successes. Sounds like something *maybe* our great-great grandmothers tried, but surely not all at once.

The methods and customs may change, but the biblical principles remain the same. The word *virtuous* implies valor, strength, a powerful force. In a marriage, what husband does not desire a faithful woman who will share her strength, willingly working beside him daily in whatever areas God gives to each of them? Whether presoaking or presiding, this woman is part of a powerful team. A godly wife doesn't seek to rule her husband and household, but to fulfill God's role as a strong helpmate, whatever responsibilities that may involve.

> *A woman who has the fear of the Lord in her heart,*
> *and the love of God in her life … has it all.*

What child doesn't long to be loved and accepted by their mother? The virtuous or godly mom may or may not design her family's wardrobe, but she can clothe her children with garments of praise and protection. She may be a one-talent woman, but she handles her resources well. Her wisdom flows not from degrees or cleverness, but from a kind and gentle heart.

This woman may not head the local charity event, but she

often makes time for hurting people around her. And she may never win a beauty contest, but she radiates the beauty of a Christ-like spirit, and her heart gives praise daily to the Maker of everything good and beautiful.

A "virtuous" woman — a strong, godly woman — is not perfect in her performance, but she is perfectly designed and accepted by God himself. And even if she feels as if she'll never measure up to this Proverbs ideal (and none of us will), her inner beauty will gain her the right kind of applause. Proverbs 31:28 says, "Her children arise and call her blessed; her husband also, and he praises her." Her greatest joy comes from the Lord himself, for "a woman who fears the LORD is to be praised" (Proverbs 31:30).

A woman who has the fear of the Lord in her heart, and the love of God in her life — has it all.

DAY-BREAK

Take time today to read Proverbs 31. What character traits do you value most? Which ones are most difficult for you? Ask God to help you work on one of those this week.

DAY-BRIEF

Charm is like a mask, and beauty doesn't last — but in God's beauty pageant, we're all queens.

DAY-VOTEDLY YOURS

God, I choose to focus on your character, your love and beauty. I admit that I can't do anything without you. You're the one I long to please. You are my ideal!

day 7
mad women

If it is possible, as far as it depends on you,
live at peace with everyone.
Romans 12:18

Ten minutes into the Bible study lesson, I knew something was wrong. Sarah, one of my two hearing-impaired students, remained unusually quiet. For about six months, the three of us had been meeting in the church auditorium "bird loft" — as we dubbed our classroom — a small space adjacent to the sound booth upstairs.

Even as a pastor's wife and church deaf interpreter, I felt totally inadequate trying to teach Sarah and Viola, both church members in their senior years. Interpreting for the deaf in the worship service and teaching one-on-one required different skills. The latter required the ability to "read" sign language in a two-way conversation — something with which I struggled. That unpolished skill and a simple misunderstanding threatened to damage my relationship as a teacher and friend with Sarah. I sensed only a divine intervention could heal it.

Our lesson text that morning centered on two women the apostle Paul had known — and possibly influenced — in the church at Philippi. According to Paul's letter, these two Christian women, Euodia and Syntyche, had been involved in a major disagreement

(Philippians 4:2 – 3). Apparently it was serious enough for Paul to enlist other believers to help these women mend their relationship. Maybe one woman had spread gossip about the other or made an unfair accusation. Perhaps deep-seated jealousy erupted, pitting one woman's giftedness against the other. Maybe it was a theological disagreement. Paul didn't explain. But whether it was pithy or pathetic, a pattern had emerged, and these two women had definitely stirred up trouble. The news reached Paul's jail cell, resulting in his firm letter. He knew the potential divisiveness of two mad women.

Most women are too relational to let disagreements fester very long.

After my Bible class ended, I questioned Sarah. At first she pretended nothing was wrong, but her body language spoke loudly. Most women are too relational to let disagreements fester very long. So I asked her if she could come early that night and meet me at the local Dairy Queen. "No agenda, just visit," I signed. Sarah acted surprised and a little reluctant, but she finally agreed.

Sarah arrived late for our meeting, but we still had time to talk before evening church services began. I eased into the problem after some small talk, and Sarah dropped her guard. Her fingers flew as she unleashed a torrent of anger and hurt. I had to sign repeatedly, "Slow down, slow down," so I could try to read her heart and her hands simultaneously.

Finally, I understood. I had not realized the subtle jealousy embedded in Sarah's heart. Her friend, Viola, was also hearing-impaired but could also talk reasonably well. She could easily reply back to me. Sarah, however, signed to me that she had no "voice." Her monotone sounds somehow made her feel inferior to Viola. She relied solely on lip-reading and sign language for understanding. Consequently, Sarah thought I had been pointing fingers at the two of them that morning in Bible study. She believed that I was accusing the two of them of fighting and that they should get along better with each other.

Relief flooded my heart as I grabbed Sarah's neck and hugged her tight. "No! No! No!" I signed. It took a half hour of explanation to convince my friend that she had misunderstood. I was so grateful that God had healed our friendship and that we had taken the time to talk.

It's a good thing I read the rest of that Philippians passage earlier that Sunday morning in Bible study — the part where Paul encouraged his readers to "Rejoice ... always ... Let your gentleness be evident to all" (Philippians 4:4 – 5). Because as Sarah and I walked back to our church nearby — she, a hearing-impaired senior, and me a young mom, smiling and laughing at the foolish misunderstanding — an approaching car slowed down alongside us near the busy intersection. The two apparently angry women in the car pointed their fingers at us and yelled out a name that ... well, I'd rather not repeat it. They obviously misunderstood — and misjudged — the action and public appearance of two Christian women friends, walking together, hand-in-hand.

I was glad Sarah couldn't hear the women's outburst, and there was no need to tell her about it. When I considered the words spewing from the car's occupants, I knew immediately this was one foolish misunderstanding only God could make right.

Some things are best left alone.

DAY-BREAK

How do you handle disagreements with others? How do you deal with your own anger?

Are there any relationships in your life that need mending? What will you do to take the first step toward bringing peace?

DAY-BRIEF

Blessed are the peacemakers, for they shall inherit many challenges.

DAY-VOTEDLY YOURS

Lord, tame my tongue and turn my heart into a listening place for others. When possible, let me be your peacemaker so others can see your love in action. Grant me the wisdom to know what to say and do. But in every situation, help me to leave the results to you.

day 8

i go to the rock

Then he went up to the temple of the LORD
and spread it out before the LORD …
"Now, LORD our God, deliver us from his hand,
so that all the kingdoms of the earth may know that you,
LORD, are the only God."

Isaiah 37:14, 20

I had just visited my gynecologist for my yearly wellness checkup. Because my doctor lives about an hour away, I always schedule a mammogram the same day. As my doctor was completing my exam he asked, "Are you scheduled for a mammogram?"

"Yes," and I named the place where I usually went.

He frowned slightly. "I want you to go to the diagnostic clinic next door. I'll see if we can get you in right away."

He didn't explain why, but hinted that something "felt a little more lumpy than usual."

The earliest appointment was still two hours away, so I had time to kill. I grabbed a sandwich nearby and munched on it in front of the clinic. My mind began to race with undisciplined thoughts: *Lord, this is where they schedule biopsies. This is where they deliver THE NEWS every woman dreads. What will my tests show?* I had always had good reports, but this appointment had been different. *What if …?*

How do you receive bad news, or even the thought of it? Fear? Worry? Panic? Withdrawal? Perhaps like me, you have struggled in the past with your initial response to crisis. Sometimes I handle major issues well, and then crumble when smaller ones come along. We know *Whom* to turn to, but we don't always go there first.

This time, I knew without a doubt what to do. When I finished eating, I opened the Bible I had brought with me in the car and began to pour out my heart to God. I turned to familiar passages of Scripture as I "spread out" the dilemma I was facing before the Lord. This situation was a small thing — but involved earth-shattering possibilities. The worst-case scenario would be every woman's nightmare.

When circumstances threaten to rock or destroy our peace, there is One alone who holds the answer.

But the more I read and prayed, the more I felt my body relax and my spirit quiet. "You're in charge, Lord," I surrendered. "It really will be all right — either way."

When circumstances threaten to rock or destroy our peace, there is One alone who holds the answer. Appealing to others may alleviate out concerns temporarily, but only as we "spread out" the situation in faith before the Lord will we see a change. It could be a change within us, like an attitude adjustment, a new declaration of faith, or the humbling of pride and our admission of weakness. But the answer will not come from within us. We need God's help.

We can offer no ultimatums, only the stark recognition that our only chance of surviving the current crisis lies in God's hands. We can ask. The rest is up to him.

What about my dilemma? Well, my appointment did require a scheduling for a biopsy, which gave me more time to again "spread out" the situation before God. But in my case, God's answer was favorable. No cancer. No problem.

I thought of others I knew whose plight was not so fortunate. Later, you'll read about Michelle, one of those women. Yet almost without fail, their declarations were the same as mine, regardless of the way God answered. While some things may have changed, one had not: they testified to God's grace and faithfulness to all who inquired.

God alone is our rock and deliverer, and when he answers, however he answers, he will orchestrate things in such a way that brings no doubt to others or us. He truly is God — and there is no other.

DAY-BREAK

When was the last time you "spread out" your questions and problems before the Lord? How did he answer you? Are you facing anything right now that threatens to steal your peace?

DAY-BRIEF

Nothing can rock our world when the Rock is in control.

DAY-VOTEDLY YOURS

God, thank you for being there in times of uncertainty and for listening to my cries. You alone are the only one who has the answers to our life dilemmas. Help me to always turn to you first to find needed help and wisdom.

think outside the box

I will pacify him with these gifts I am sending on ahead;
later, when I see him, perhaps he will receive me.
Genesis 32:20

Lodged in Jacob's memory was the red face of his brother Esau whom he had betrayed years earlier. Jacob probably replayed the scenario a hundred times through the years, even though he escaped without ever experiencing his brother Esau's rage.

Twice Jacob deceived his brother. The first time, he tricked Esau out of his birthright with a pot of stew. And the second time, following his mother's instructions, Jacob stole his brother's blessing after disguising himself as Esau in the presence of his blind father. Esau's grudge against Jacob festered into a full-blown plot to kill his brother, but before he could take action, Jacob left the country.

Jacob married, and the years came and went. He finally tired of living around an uncle who continually tried to deceive him, so Jacob ultimately decided to return home with his multiplied family, servants, and livestock.

On the way back home, fear paralyzed Jacob when he discovered Esau was coming to meet him with a band of four hundred men. All Jacob could focus on was what he had done to Esau, the brother he betrayed, the sibling who hated him enough to kill him. Not knowing how Esau still felt, Jacob tried to appease his brother with gifts. He offered herds of livestock and even sent his wives and children over first, perhaps to soften the blow a bit. Jacob was caught in a time warp. All he could visualize were the circumstances as he once knew them. He never considered that things could have changed. In his mind, Jacob had created a box of his own making, and he had put Esau in the middle of it (Genesis 25 – 31).

We women too, at one time or another, may have done the same thing. Scarred by a painful encounter or event or afraid of a friend or relative's behavior, we've coped by placing them in a box. We've built a mental, four-walled cubicle that has encased every harsh word, every heated argument, and every injustice we — or they — ever committed. Five, maybe twenty years pass. But in our thoughts, the memories are as fresh as yesterday. And the thought of reconnecting with them leaves us petrified, or at least skeptical. Does it sound like a modern-day Hallmark movie plot?

> **Freeing people from our self-made boxes may not change them — but it will help change us.**

We may prefer withdrawal, disconnects, or pretense, but when it seems certain the meeting will take place again, our emotions refuse to budge. They stay locked in the past.

Maybe they've changed. Haven't I changed? After all, it's been a long time. It's water under the bridge. I'm sure they have forgotten.

Thoughts like these can't find an opening in our box, because we've wedged the past too tightly inside.

Imagine our surprise, like Jacob, when Esau sees his brother in the distance and eagerly runs to hug him. Think of all the time Jacob wasted worrying and fretting about something that never happened.

Time won't dissolve the walls of our emotional boxes, and it's not time that changes people's hearts. Not really. Thinking — and acting — outside the box is risky, and it usually costs something: time, effort, persistence, and possibly pride. Only God can break down the barriers of fear and distrust.

You may be thinking, *The wounds are too deep. You don't know my family. You don't know what happened. What if they don't respond like Esau?*

You may be right. But what if they do?

Bribery doesn't work, and fear accomplishes nothing. You can only do your part. Freeing people from our self-made boxes may not change them — but it will help change us. Life is too short and love is too powerful not to make the best of both. What you see as impossible, God may not only see as possible, but necessary. His help is always available.

God could have left us inside a "box" — imprisoned by our own sin. But he loved us too much to permanently sever the relationship he first began. Jacob wanted to pacify Esau. God wanted to pursue us. God did his part. He willingly sent his own Son to break down the walls forever. It wasn't bribery. It was — and is — a gift. The rest is up to us.

When we respond positively and throw away the "boxes," the new relationship with God — and others — is forever worth the price of that gift.

DAY-BREAK

Think about any difficult relationships or situations from the past. Have you placed anyone in a box of your own choosing, based on the past? How can you "think outside the box" and began visualizing change in yourself and in others? What steps will you take to make the first move toward reconciliation and renew the relationship?

DAY-BRIEF

Only the lonely live in self-made boxes.

DAY-VOTEDLY YOURS

Father, fill my thoughts with possibilities, not failures. Teach me how to forgive, and free me from any prisons of distrust or fear I may have built. Love through me so that others might know you.

day 10
holy socks

Oh, that you would bless me and enlarge my territory!
1 Chronicles 4:10

The young Christian woman was eager to begin her assignment. "I just want to bless their socks off," she bubbled. The woman had agreed to her appearing on *Trading Spouses*, a Fox reality show in which two families, usually of different social classes, swap wives or husbands for a week. Each family is awarded $50,000, with the stipulation that the guest mother decides how her host family must spend the money.[1] During the time of the monitored experiment, the two women would exert their gifts and influence within the respective families.

But neither woman knew the challenges waiting for them. In this particular episode, the other woman involved, of a non-religious persuasion, couldn't understand the need for so much Bible study, church attendance, and "fellowship" time with other Christians, a core practice of her temporary, surrogate family. When she finally agreed to attend a women's Bible study, she grew fidgety and uncomfortable and left early. After the experiment was over, she returned home eager to resume her own lifestyle.

In her attempt to bring "Sonshine" to her substitute family, the Christian woman encountered another set of standards as well, along with a lack of enthusiasm. When she reunited with her own family, her emotions gave way to a torrent of tears. I'm sure she couldn't understand why some people wouldn't want to wear blessed socks.

The truth is, not everyone wants — or comprehends what it means — to be blessed. Content in their own comfort zones, some women can't imagine altering their lifestyles.

Forcing our beliefs or desires on others may result only in driving them away. After all, we are only the channels of blessing. God is the ultimate Blessing Giver. And he is the rewarder of those who earnestly seek him, not those who reject his offer (Hebrews 11:6). Although his generosity and love extend to the entire world, God doesn't bless those who would just as soon keep their socks on.

God is the ultimate Blessing Giver.

Even Christian women can misunderstand God's grace, power, and desire to bless. God's Word overflows with blessings of obedience, joy, relationship, character, and provision. Yet many never receive them. Why?

Bruce Wilkinson, in his popular book *The Prayer of Jabez*, says, "God's bounty is limited only by us, not by His resources, power, or willingness to give. Jabez was blessed simply because he refused to let any obstacle, person, or opinion loom larger than God's nature. And God's nature is to bless."[2]

Bruce shares a fable about a man who dies and goes to heaven. He notices an odd-looking warehouse and asks Peter about it. Against Peter's caution, the man rushes into the building and discovers endless shelves of ribbon-wrapped boxes. He sees one with his name on it, but is immediately filled with regret as he views the contents — all the unclaimed blessings God wanted to give the man while he was on earth.

Bruce points out how sad it is to come to the end of our lives and discover all the blessings God wanted to give us, but we never received — because we never asked.[3]

Ephesians 3:20 gives us a small picture of how God wants to bless us: "Now to him who is able to do immeasurably more than all we ask or imagine, according to his power that is at work within us …"

In our own strength, we can't convince others to receive God's blessings. But as we patiently share the goodness of God with them, with time and prayer, perhaps God will give them a tiny glimpse into his storehouse — so they will ultimately seek to know him for themselves.

DAY-BREAK

How has God blessed you? In what areas do you need to trust God more? How are you sharing his blessings? Start asking God to bless you however, wherever, and whenever he wants, so that you, in turn, can bless him and others. As you read his Word daily, circle or list the promises God has made to you if you are his child, and any conditions accompanying them.

DAY-BRIEF

Even the blind can recognize daily blessings from God, if they see with eyes of faith.

DAY-VOTEDLY YOURS

Lord, give me a clean heart — and clean socks. Then fill them with every blessing that has my name on it. Help me to choose obedience continually so I can always be a channel of blessing for others.

the great cover-up

Whoever would foster love covers over an offense,
but whoever repeats the matter separates close friends.
Proverbs 17:9

Macy opened her textbook and asked for a volunteer. "Okay, class. Who can quote their multiplication tables?"

In school, repetition may be a good teacher. Two plus two equals four. Five times six equals thirty. Eight times nine equals seventy-two. Rehearse your facts and numbers enough times and the brain registers the answers. Voila!

But what about life? Repeating certain actions not only discourages learning; it actually encourages discontent and loneliness. Someone who chooses continually to offend, to hurt, to lash out against another with little regard for the other's welfare or feelings, won't gain a reputation for making friends. Just the opposite. Who wants to be the target of someone's repetitive anger?

Nevertheless, in our hearts and hands is the God-given power to help turn all that around. We all encounter seemingly impossible people in our lives — those whose purpose in life seems bent on making others miserable. No matter how hard we try to confront or ignore them, nothing changes.

Only God can truly change a heart. But as women, when we

refuse to retaliate against that "irregular" person, we are choosing to "cover" another with God's grace. We are not called to ignore the offense, only to cover it.

If we're wise, we won't walk out in a thunderstorm unprepared with no umbrella. But when we walk under the protection of a loving God whose forgiving heart reaches out and pursues even the unlovely and unkind, we become coworkers with him who called us not to hate, but to love.

Only God can change a heart.

We face a choice: we too can be repeaters. When others turn on us, we can repeatedly chasten, ignore, or tear down the other person in a spirit of revenge. But genuine love doesn't retaliate or hold grudges. When the unkindness of another splatters on us, we can choose to lovingly hold out an umbrella — over them and us — to cover their actions. Someone once said, "Forgiveness is the quality of heart that forgets the injury and forgives the offender."[4]

Forgiving love not only covers an offense. It may even help to free the trapped offender.

DAY-BREAK

Think about the "irregular" people in your life. Pray for them by name. Think of one positive quality about each one and compliment them the next time you see them.

DAY-BRIEF

A friend is someone who lets you share her umbrella.

DAY-VOTEDLY YOURS

God, your love has covered my offenses once and for all. Teach me how to love others even when their behavior is anything but lovely. And remind me often if I forget how to forgive.

a woman's choice

I will allow no sleep to my eyes
or slumber to my eyelids,
till I find a place for the LORD,
a dwelling for the Mighty One of Jacob.

Psalm 132:4 – 5

For years I struggled with restlessness in my spirit. I kept asking God for help. I wasn't sure what I needed, but my life felt cluttered. Activity and obligations seemed to fill every moment. When my husband's job change resulted in a move to a smaller town, I thought, *This is my answer. I can downsize and find a cute place where I can decorate to my heart's content.*

We did downsize, and I set to work plotting out my new décor. But in the middle of my decorating frenzy, God whispered to my spirit, "This isn't what you need. I know the source of your restlessness. It's in your heart. Let me redesign and simplify your heart. We'll eliminate the clutter. I'll walk with you through your home and remind you again of what's really important. When I'm finished, this will be not a house, but a beautiful home where my presence will abide with you daily."

God yearns to be at home in your heart.

Maybe you've felt that same restlessness. Life is a constant flurry of activity and filled with choices. Whether you're single or married, young or old, a woman's life, like the contents of a home, fills up quickly. Some women stuff their lives with people, leaving no discretionary down time. Others add commitments like furniture crammed into every nook and cranny of their homes. Too many yeses, too few nos, and time slips away. Is there room for the Lord somewhere? Or does something or someone occupy every space?

Like Jesus' words whispered to me, David's words encourage us to keep searching, not to give up in despair. Although God did not allow him to build a temple, a permanent "dwelling place" on earth to replace the tabernacle structure, that didn't change his resolve or his longing. God appointed David's son Solomon to construct the actual building. But David himself kept the reputation of being a "man after [God's] own heart" (Acts 13:22).

What would happen if we, like David, determined not to rest or sleep until we found a suitable place for the King of kings to take up residence in our hearts — giving him first-throne rights? How would our lives change if we were willing to keep emptying the clutter to make room for him?

God won't force his way into any life. But he longs to find a permanent dwelling place in you. He yearns to be at home in your heart.

The choice is yours.

DAY-BREAK

Perhaps Jesus is looking for a place to be born in your heart, for the very first time. If so, what will you say as he comes knocking?

If your life is so full that you've crowded out the Lord's presence, how can you make room for him again? What steps will you take this week?

DAY-BRIEF

In God's home, there's always room for his children.

DAY-VOTEDLY YOURS

Lord, help me rearrange the furniture in my heart and eliminate the "clutter" of my life — whatever is taking up useless and unnecessary space. I want to make room for what's important in life, especially for that permanent dwelling place in my heart for you.

day 13

renovation time

Being confident of this, that he who began a good work in you
will carry it on to completion until the day of Christ Jesus.
Philippians 1:6

In the process of redoing my children's bedroom one year, I decided to refinish their chest of drawers to match the rest of the room décor. That piece of furniture had been in our family for some time, so it was fairly worn.

I thought some minor sanding would probably suffice, but a few minor chips remained that were too difficult to smooth. Ultimately, I decided to strip the entire surface to the bare wood.

What started out as a simple project took several weeks to complete. As the paint began to peel off, I discovered not just one, but three coats underneath. The more I chipped and scrubbed, the clearer I could see a beautiful stained wood surface underneath. Once the layers disappeared, painting was easy: no lumps, bumps, or unevenly colored surfaces to hinder my progress.

God never gets in a hurry,
and he never abandons the work he has started.

As women, we may feel like that piece of furniture. We come to Jesus in need of renovation, and he does not disappoint us. The

Master Designer and Painter begins to strip and sand down the layers that have built up. The process seems endless, and we see only ugliness and hopelessness at times. But Jesus visualizes the potential. Patiently, little by little, he peels away the coats: scars of sin, accumulation of fears, and the inconsistencies of our own selfish nature. When he finishes the sanding, the surface underneath is smooth to the touch.

Now he is ready to start the new work: repainting and refashioning our lives to match the "décor" of his own character. At times we may feel dull and useless, with our lumps and bumps showing through. Life ticks by, dreams fade, and we grow older. Is God truly making something useful of our lives? But God's work is the finest, and as we simply yield to his hands, he'll create something beautiful again, something fit for our priceless home in heaven. I think of the process this way:

> *Long after the colors of life have dulled,*
> *And the glitter has faded from view,*
> *The shine of your face grows brighter still —*
> *As we see the beauty of You.*
> *Long after the accolades are gone,*
> *And the crowds have reduced to a few,*
> *And all of life's dreams have passed away,*
> *What remains is the beauty of You.*

God never gets in a hurry, and he never abandons the work he has started. The complete renovation may take a lifetime. In his own way he works carefully and creatively. But when he finishes, his workmanship truly has the heavenly seal of approval: "That's good!" What remains is a true reflection of his own beauty.

DAY-BREAK

Have you ever felt like that piece of furniture? Where do you think your life is in that renovation process? Stripping? Sanding? Repainting? Is his reflection showing yet?

DAY-BRIEF

When God finishes a work, it's always good.

DAY-VOTEDLY YOURS

Lord, thank you for never giving up on me. Keep working on my character until it shines with your beauty.

oceans of love

Many waters cannot quench love; rivers cannot sweep it away.
Song of Songs 8:7

Each year when the buds appeared on the mulberry trees, the ministerial staff of our former church escaped for a week of recreation together at Lake Obregon, Mexico. At that time, there were no cell phones, and their tents were pitched far from city phone lines. As wives, we had no clue of their safety or whereabouts — until we saw them walk through the front door a week later. Needless to say, we relied greatly on prayer during those trips.

For weeks ahead, you could probably find the men — including my husband — holed up in their garages — polishing their reels, untangling line, sharpening hooks, and gloating over the big bass they were sure would top their record from the previous year.

Endless trips to nearby sporting goods stores to choose the best and newest lures, sorting and re-sorting a dozen varieties of colored worms and plastic lizards, and a wide grin on each face — all characterized the men's pretrip ritual.

Our pastor at that time had developed a reputation for quick exits from church on Sunday night before the big fishing excursion. During a pastor-appointed, benediction prayer, the staff would disappear. Years later, on our pastor's tenth anniversary celebration, the staff presented him with an unusual memento: at the front of the church, someone slid in a grinning, life-sized, cardboard replica of Pastor Don, waving good-bye to the congregation, reminiscent of those infamous journeys to Mexico.

We assumed on each trip that the men were in good hands and having a great time. But one year, tragedy almost struck. My husband Larry related the story after returning home.

The men rarely stopped to rest after their all-night journey into Mexico's interior. As soon as they saw water, they cranked up the boats and headed out. On the first day, Larry and his partner headed several miles up the lake to a favorite spot. The fishing was good, and when it was time to call it a day, they decided to fish just a little longer. Soon they began to notice the increasing winds. The waves were white-capping and battering the small fourteen-foot bass boat.

As they started across the open water, waves began to lap over the bow, and soon they found themselves in knee-deep water and bailing like crazy. It was too late. The boat capsized, and rods, tackle boxes, and the rest of the boat's contents went to the bottom of the lake. The men were able to grab the side of the boat and hang on.

Clinging to the sides of the boat in the murky water and the diminishing daylight, their knuckles the color of the white caps, the two men tried to encourage each other. "Maybe, just maybe there's another boat still out here." That's when the prayer meeting began. They cried out to God for someone — anyone — to come and help.

Within five minutes, they saw a faint light and the unmistakable sound of a boat motor. Soon the USS *Heavenly Angel* (or so they could have christened it), with two fishermen aboard, pulled up alongside the boat's hull and rescued the two shivering men.

Did that close encounter dampen their spirits? Not on your life. With a good night's sleep and borrowed gear, they headed back out the next day for more fishing adventures — this time returning before the afternoon winds began to howl.

Insurance paid for the loss of Larry's valuable fishing equipment, but no amount of money could have covered the pain had I lost my precious husband. The incident didn't eliminate his love for fishing — and only strengthened our love for a Savior who cared enough to send my husband a special escort back to shore. But that night also reminded me of a saying I once read, paraphrased: "Let your parting always be sweet, with spoken words of love."

Let your parting always be sweet,
with spoken words of love.

Jesus' personal touch that night in the middle of the lake changed my perspective as a woman and as a wife. Hugs-on-the-run and quick, "cardboard" good-bye waves would never suffice after that encounter. Our God-given, deep-down peace and love for each other began to grow in oceanic proportions.

And although typical marriage misunderstandings and conflicts have threatened to "rock the boat" and overturn our marriage at times, now we rarely, if ever, leave each other's presence without a lingering expression that says, "I love you — for always."

DAY-BREAK

When a loved one leaves your presence, whether for a short or extended time, how do you say good-bye? Have you ever experienced an anxious situation where a loved one's life was spared? How did God help you through it?

DAY-BRIEF

Whether starting or parting, life — and people — are special gifts to treasure.

DAY-VOTEDLY YOURS

Lord, thank you for all the times you intervened and sent guardian angels to watch over and protect us. Thank you for the special relationships you bring into our lives. Teach us how to treasure them as special gifts from you.

the early bird gets the words

For where your treasure is, there your heart will be also.
Matthew 6:21

My name is Rebecca Jordan, and I am a bargain-aholic. At least I used to be. I could smell a bargain before the word *sale* ever hit the papers. In those days, instead of buying one or two decorative baskets from a garage sale, I'd tote home twenty. "They were so cheap!" I'd rationalize. "And just look at these great shapes."

I grew up in a family of bargain hunters. I can still see images of my dad walking down the alley toward our house, wagging home some useable discard he'd rescued from a nearby dumpster. And I learned from my mom to spot antique bargains at garage sales. Occasionally with her help, I managed to make a small profit from reselling them — enough to keep me going back for more. Most of the time, however, I didn't seem to have her knack of knowing when to "hold 'em and when to fold 'em." I just knew how to hold 'em.

I also discovered that if you wanted to find the best bargains at garage sales, you had to swoop in as soon as the sale opened, if not before. Each time I went, which was often, I plotted my treasure hunt carefully, placing a star by the best sales in the newspaper and circling the addresses. And usually I'd find a special treasure or two if I beat the antique dealers to the prized spots.

One time in particular I turned onto a tree-lined street and saw a garage sale sign, complete with red and yellow balloons waving freely in the breeze, and no shoppers in sight. *A virgin sale!*

I raced out of the car and couldn't believe my eyes. A quick scan of the tables revealed piles of goodies, just waiting to be devoured like choice worms in a garden. I found an empty box and began filling it with antique glassware pieces, along with other assorted treasures.

After about twenty minutes, my box bulging with super finds, I headed for the checkout table. Out of the corner of my eye, I saw a lady sprinting from her car. Within a few seconds, I heard a familiar voice. The woman looked at my box and said with more than a little sarcasm, "Well, did you leave anything for me?" She was one of our church members, an avid antique collector, and a woman with a reputation for many words — not all of which were complimentary.

In my spirit, I seemed to hear God whispering, "Did you leave any treasures for me?"

I stood there wishing I were the canary that the cat had swallowed. I wanted to disappear — anywhere. "I'm sure you can still find a few bargains," I replied meekly. And then I plopped my money on the table and hurried off to my other destinations.

By the time I completed my rounds, the back seat of the car was piled high with secondhand treasures. But as I unpacked them one by one and began looking around in my house for a prominent place to showcase my purchases, an uncomfortable feeling crept in and stole my joy. At first I thought maybe God was trying to teach me a lesson: *Don't compete with church members at garage sales.* But I wasn't trying to compete. I just happened to arrive at the sale before she did. I soon discovered God had something else in mind.

I had already stuffed my cabinets to capacity. In order to find a place for these new treasures, I would either need to discard some things, or build another storage room like the rich man in Jesus' parable (Luke 12:16 – 18). In my spirit, I seemed to hear God whispering, "Did you leave any treasures for me?" I knew exactly what he meant.

I no longer scour garage sales for bargains to resell. For the last few years, I've been trying to downsize instead and give other bargain hunters a chance at "the hunt." But I still enjoy finding a good keeper occasionally, whether at a department store or someone's backyard sale. What can I say? I'm a woman. I'll always love a good bargain, and being a collector is in my family genes to stay.

But should that tendency get out of control and I start stuffing my life full of too many useless things, I try to remember that church member's words — and the gentle prodding of my heavenly Father, reminding me of my priorities once again.

DAY-BREAK

What are your treasures? Where do you keep them? What kind of "treasures" are you laying up for eternity?

DAY-BRIEF

The pleasure of real treasure is in knowing it all belongs to God.

DAY-VOTEDLY YOURS

Lord, when priorities shift, remind me of what and where my real treasures are. Teach me how to value the right things. Thank you, Lord, for being the greatest treasure of all.

day 16
ministry is people

Love your neighbor as yourself.
James 2:8

Our house had sold quickly in the Dallas metroplex where we lived for almost ten years — so quickly that we were unable to find another home to buy before closing the sale. So we rented for about four months in a small rural community on the edge of East Texas, about fifteen miles from my husband's new employment.

After the move, most of my transplanted roses and other flowers still stood languishing in pots, awaiting their final destination. One hot summer morning I had just moved some of them to the front yard and was popping off the heads of some spent daisies. From down the street I heard someone hollering, "Whatcha doin'?"

I ignored her at first, thinking she was talking to someone else.

But again the voice of an elderly woman yelled, "Whatcha doin'?" By this time, she had walked halfway across the dirt road in front of my house. "Come on over and visit. Sit down a while."

"Well, I really need to ..." I started to say "work," but she interrupted me.

"I'll get a chair. Come sit down!"

As women we can always find reasons for justifying our busyness, whether we live in the city or country. Living in a Dallas city suburb didn't exactly make me a veteran when it came to neighborly visits. Like, who has the time? As a minister's wife, much of my energy centered on church activities, family, and writing. I knew a few of my neighbors by first name, but I rarely visited in their homes. When a moving van would roll up to a nearby house, at least I tried to greet the new family at their front door with an apple pie.

But here in the "country," as I rehearsed my excuses for not crossing the street, the words of a city friend of mine, Kris Brown, kept ringing in my ears: "Ministry is people." I recognized the words not as an accusation leading to false guilt, but as a prompting of the Holy Spirit. *What good does it do to write about loving my neighbor if I don't practice it myself?*

> ### *What good does it do to write about loving my neighbor if I don't practice it myself?*

I could think of no good excuses to offer the woman in my new surroundings, so I accepted her invitation. After all, I had wanted to meet the people around me. And it had been a while since I had baked a pie for a neighbor. (Of course *I* was the new neighbor this time.) However, I soon realized this lady and her invalid husband sitting in her driveway didn't need something to feed their stomachs. They wanted food for the soul. They were lonely.

I sat down and made a weak attempt to start our conversation. "This is a nice place to live."

"No, it's not!" the woman replied sharply. "People just stay in their houses and never come outside to check on you if you're sick or anything."

I hoped she couldn't see the guilt creeping over my face at that moment. But after all, I reasoned, my husband had helped them one night with a minor repair. I just hadn't had time to go over ... busy ... gone ... housework ... writing ... church ... three dogs.

Suddenly I saw a flashback of the Samaritan who stopped to help the wounded man when no one else had time (Luke 10:30 – 37). My constant prayers of "Lord, make me useable; order my steps today" stuck in my throat.

I stayed and talked for almost an hour. And I must admit, it was one of the most refreshing moments I'd experienced in a long time.

As I returned home to finish tending my plants that day, I whispered another prayer: "Soon, Lord, you will transplant me and root me in solid ground, in a permanent home in town. But until then, like these roses and daisies sunning in the front yard of my temporary home, I will bloom here — for however long you want."

Hmm. My neighbor's birthday is next month ... Maybe I could make another visit — and bake a birthday pie?

DAY-BREAK

How many of your neighbors do you know? What can you do this week to encourage someone in your neighborhood?

DAY-BRIEF

Wherever there is love, there is a neighbor waiting to receive it.

DAY-VOTEDLY YOURS

Lord, open my eyes to the people around me, especially those who live in my neighborhood. Show me unique ways to show your love and your light to those who need it most.

it's not my gift!

This kind can come out by nothing but prayer and fasting.
Mark 9:29 NKJV

A woman in our church had been asking to talk with me, but the connection just wasn't happening. One day after church she approached me again, and I said, "You know what? Let's just take time now. Do you have a minute?"

We sat down on the steps leading to the church baptistery, where we wouldn't be disturbed. The young mom began to share. I was not a trained counselor, yet women often sought me out. As a minister's wife, I knew my limitations and simply offered a listening ear for those who needed to talk.

Most of the time I ended up using my spiritual gifts: mercy, teaching, or encouragement. I usually tried to identify with the other person's hurts and joys and encourage as best I could, or I attempted to "teach" them what they could do to get through their difficulties. Counseling was not my "gift." Occasionally, I would be bold enough to speak a word of correction, but after some bad attempts, I learned that I must earn the right and respect to do that, and only when God was the One prompting me to do so in love.

But this woman's problems sounded simple, and she talked to me about common, surface issues. At that time in my life I was not skilled in probing for deeper issues. I left that to my husband, a pastor and counselor. As I've grown older, God has often given me words of discernment to share with women, but at the time, I was not much older than this woman. For some reason, I had few such words to offer.

She spoke of busy schedules, trouble focusing on main things — the usual complaints of women her age. After listening to her rambling comments for half an hour, I finally encouraged her to "just say no" to excess commitments, to ask for God's guidance, and to ease up some on her schedule. I prayed with her, and she left. I didn't feel too confident at my attempts to help, but I didn't know what else to say. I promised to keep praying for her, and I did.

Weeks later the phone rang. I heard my husband's voice, a little edgy, "Honey, can you come to my office? I need your help." He shared with me that he was talking to the same woman with whom I had met a few weeks earlier, and he felt uneasy about how the session was going. He thought she might be physically ill.

I walked into Larry's office, and at first the woman's behavior seemed normal as we exchanged greetings. Then with no warning she began to shake violently. Her eyes took on a glazed look, as arms and legs flailed wildly. Larry and I both tried to calm her, but the force of her strength was phenomenal. That's when we knew her problem was probably not a physical one.

We both looked at each other with a sense of helplessness, realizing we were dealing with a level of spiritual warfare that was bigger than our experience. But we knew Someone who could help.

We began crying out to God. Finally, after what seemed like an eternity, the woman became silent, and her body grew still. Then she opened her eyes as if nothing had happened.

We talked with her for a while, prayed for her again, and then encouraged her to seek out a professional Christian counselor. It was obvious her needs were substantial. She later began attending a neighboring church in our town and we lost track of her.

A couple of years later I ran into the woman at a community event, and she looked radiant. Her eyes sparkled with confidence as she told about finding a woman counselor who had experience with her problems. She related how through much prayer and working with her, the counselor had guided her to spiritual freedom. She had even become involved in a special ministry that helped others overcome spiritual bondage.

> *God may use someone else's gifts to free a person*
> *from long-standing spiritual warfare,*
> *but he will also use our prayers, any way he wants.*

That experience taught me something about the futility of quick fixes and the power of fervent prayer. When other women approach us for help, we don't have to cry, "Can't help. It's not my gift!" But neither should we rely on our human efforts to solve others' problems. As a woman, I was not wrong in trying to help. Even Jesus' disciples failed in their attempts to help someone and complained to Jesus, "How come our efforts didn't work?" (Mark 9:28, author's paraphrase). But there is more we can do.

Spiritual strongholds sometimes attach themselves so deeply in others' lives that only the disciplines of sacrificial prayer and fasting will bring God's deliverance. Our children, our friends, our families — and those whom God purposely brings into our lives — need our prayers.

God needs women who know the difference between quick repairs and permanent freedom — women who find power, not from their own limited knowledge, but on their knees. God may use someone else's gifts and training to free a person from long-standing spiritual warfare, but he will also use our prayers, any way he wants.

Prayer *is* a gift — but it's a gift we can all give away.

DAY-BREAK

Have you ever cried, "That's not my gift"? What do you usually say to women who come to you with problems? What resources are available to you? What are you doing with your "gift" of prayer?

DAY-BRIEF

Praying is the habit of staying — connected to God's power.

DAY-VOTEDLY YOURS

Lord Jesus, my gifts and my knowledge are so limited. But you are so powerful. Thank you for this privilege and discipline of prayer. Teach me how to pray more effectively — and more sacrificially.

day 18

you can do it!

I can do all this through him who gives me strength.
Philippians 4:13

One year I flew out to see my mom and help take care of her after she broke her hip. For several days I pampered her, painting her nails, cooking meals, cleaning house, and watching old movie reruns with her. She was cautious about walking and still fearful of falling again.

Before I left, I bundled her in the car so we could go see the doctor for a follow-up appointment. The doctor removed her staples and then said, "You can walk on that leg all you want now. Move as quickly as you can from the walker to the cane."

Mom was a gifted pianist, but the accident had kept her away from the piano for some time. The doctor's words worked like magic. As soon as we got home, she fairly flew over to the piano, scooted the seat back, and began to play just like she did before the accident. Those affirmative words from the doctor were like music to my mother's ears — and hearing her play had the same effect on me.

Every day we will cross paths with others who are just waiting for someone to give them permission to move ahead, to throw away their walkers — their excuses — and start running again.

Paralyzed by one too many failures, they've lost the desire to even try again.

Haven't you experienced times of crippling fear when you literally couldn't put one foot in front of the other? Times when the beating of your heart drowned out the beat of the music within your spirit?

At those moments what women need most is more than an empathetic ear, though that helps too. But sometimes they need a gentle push. God has already provided the healing, but they hold on to their emotional or physical walkers, afraid to trust, afraid to move forward.

> *Every day we will cross paths with others*
> *who are just waiting for someone to give them*
> *permission to move ahead, to throw away their*
> *walkers — their excuses — and start running again.*

Sometimes, they are just waiting for someone to give them permission to forge ahead — and the words, "You can do it."

That's where you come in. Be gentle. Be encouraging. But be firm. Add the two words ("through Christ") that will pave the way. Invite them to throw away their walkers and venture out into a faith walk, prodding them on with "Through Christ, you can do it!"

There's more than just magic in those words. Because when they come to believe it themselves, it's like music to the ears and strength to the soul.

DAY-BREAK

When was the last time someone gave you a gentle push or an affirmative nod of confidence to help you through tough times? Whom will you encourage this week?

DAY-BRIEF

The key to our strength is tapping into his.

DAY-VOTEDLY YOURS

Jesus, thank you for giving me the strength to try all things and to do all things. Help me to be the kind of encourager that others need.

day 19
bendable but dependable

For though the righteous fall seven times, they rise again …
Proverbs 24:16

Someone once said our only real failure is when we fail to try, for success is built on failure.

Often when we think about a biblical example of failure, even women instantly identify with Peter. Peter's brash impulsiveness led him into one problem after another as he consistently acted before he thought. Who was it that wanted to go walking on the water to Jesus and almost sank out of fear during the process? Peter (Matthew 14:28 – 30).

And which disciple whacked off the ear of the servant of the high priest, who was with the band trying to take Jesus by force? Right again, Peter (John 18:10). And who totally bombed out and denied Jesus three times, just when Jesus needed him the most? Yes, it was Peter, the "rock" who experienced bitter failure (Luke 22:54 – 62).

However, most of our identification with this foolhardy disciple stops there, unless you can also claim another quality that fit Peter: resiliency. Some of you may remember that strange-looking toy a few decades ago that children could twist, pull, and bend — and its arms would always spring back to their original shape. That unusual toy was known as "Stretch Armstrong," and kids loved it.

That was Peter. He failed — again and again — and was stretched out of shape because of fear, impulsiveness, and carelessness. Yet in spite of Peter's negative qualities, perhaps his positive characteristics — such as an adventurous spirit and a protective nature — affected his decisions too. At least he was willing to *try* walking out to Jesus. All the other disciples stayed in the boat. And at first, when Jesus was being arrested, Peter wanted to do something, anything, to keep Jesus from harm.

Jesus specializes in transforming weaknesses into strengths.

And at least Peter bounced back. The book of Acts is filled with Peter's boldness after the coming of the Holy Spirit. Even death proved his fierce, resilient commitment. In spite of his earlier, consistent failures, tradition tells us this disciple died upside down on a cross because he felt unworthy to die like his beloved Master.

Has failure dogged your life? Does it seem as if everything you touch turns to ashes? Jesus specializes in transforming weaknesses into strengths (2 Corinthians 12:9). He doesn't break a "bruised reed" (Isaiah 42:3). And he longs to give you the beauty of resiliency.

All of us may feel stretched beyond recognition at times. Everyone fails — or falls — at one time or another. Some give up, but winners rise and bounce back.

Which one are you?

DAY-BREAK

What has failure taught you? How have you bounced back from past mistakes or failures? How can you encourage someone this week to develop resiliency in her life?

DAY-BRIEF

It's not how many times you fall, but how many times you get up that matters.

DAY-VOTEDLY YOURS

Jesus, you have picked me up so many times when I've fallen. How can I thank you for never giving up on me? Use my failures and flaws as a springboard to help others, and keep teaching me resiliency.

day 20

i wish you could hear

How beautiful are the feet of those who bring good news!
Romans 10:15

The week before Easter one year, our pastor's wife presented a beautiful and moving presentation in song about the crucifixion of Christ. At one point, the taped background played voices at the trial and crucifixion. Sounds of angry mockers swelled with intensity: "Crucify him! Crucify him!"

I was interpreting for Sarah, one of the hearing-impaired women who attended our church. In the dimly lit auditorium Sarah could barely see my hands and face, and it was extremely difficult to communicate in sign language the musical drama playing out before us.

I was doing fairly well until the music suddenly stopped. During the most intense moments of that pause, I tried to convey the thundering noise of the pounding hammer I heard, as if it were driving the spikes into the hands of Jesus.

Tears began to trickle down my cheeks as I signed, "Oh, I wish you could hear! I wish you could hear!" in utter frustration. Then I tried to explain to Sarah what was happening as I alternately pounded each fist into my other outstretched hand. She grabbed a hymnal in front of her and placed one hand flat on it, palm side down — an action that often helped her to feel the vibrations of loud sounds or heavy music beats.

A few minutes later, in Sarah's own way and with nimble fingers, she signed, "God knows, God knows. It's all right. I understand."

Have you struggled with sharing your faith? Afraid you can't communicate well? Sometimes, we build our own barriers with excuses like "I don't know the Bible well enough"; "We don't speak the same language"; "We have nothing in common"; "It's too hard"; or "They probably won't understand."

Physical barriers never limit God's Spirit.

Physical barriers never limit God's Spirit. The story of Jesus has traveled through prison walls and across enemy lines. It's survived ocean shipwrecks and disastrous earthquakes. It has seeped through secret tunnels and hidden caves, and it has found its way into the hearts of women like you and me. Since the creation of the world, God has been revealing himself and his message, and it has been clearly seen and understood (Romans 1:20).

Sarah couldn't "hear," yet she "heard" the message without my speaking a word. If God can help a hearing-impaired woman understand the heart of the gospel through some vibrations on a songbook, will he not also tear down whatever obstacle we envision? Instead of *wishing* others could hear, we have the privilege of helping them find a way to listen. Our actions, our lifestyles, our beliefs, the words we speak, and even the words we don't say, all communicate the truths within our hearts and in his Word.

But where do we find them — people who need to "hear"? Look around you: in the doctor's office, on the subway, in the restaurant, or a grocery line. You'll find them next to you in an airplane or a work cubicle, at the soccer field, or in the home next door. People are always watching — and listening. God will do his part to prepare their hearts. But we must also prepare ours.

If we are willing, he will use us and make a way for others to truly hear — and understand — the good news.

DAY-BREAK

What opportunities has God given you lately to share the good news about Jesus? Ask the Lord to open your eyes and your heart this week to others who might not know him.

DAY-BRIEF

What God gives, we must share.

DAY-VOTEDLY YOURS

Lord, forgive me for the times when I remain silent or make excuses instead of honoring the name of Jesus, and when I seem deaf to the needs of others. Let my cry always ring out with the consuming desire of "Let me tell you about my Jesus!"

day 21
spice it up!

Do not neglect your gift …
1 Timothy 4:14

"Honey, you forgot the salt!"

Jane agreed with her husband as soon as she tasted the hot soup she had just placed on the kitchen table. Rummaging through the cabinets, she grabbed the saltshaker to revive her concoction.

"Perfect," they both said in unison, as they each tried a new spoonful.

God made us unique as women. There's no one else exactly like you! Just like the spices in a good recipe add up to a great dish, our spices, or gifts, add rich flavor to our world, particularly to the body of Christ — other believers (1 Corinthians 12).

But what gifts to use and how God develops those spices often mystify us. Some of us spend a lifetime trying to figure out where we fit in: "What's my spice? How do I use it?"

God created all of us with one general spice in mind. In Matthew 5:13 Jesus calls us the "salt of the earth." If we aren't using our "salt" to season the world and attract people to Jesus, what good does it do? The Bible says we were created on purpose for his purpose (Colossians 1:16, author's paraphrase). Think of that purpose as our salt — our universal spice — giving glory to God.

But then God weaves into our recipe some very special spices that fit us alone. We are born with natural gifts, like athletic bodies, business minds, practical skills, or musical abilities. When we become God's children and are "born again" (John 3:3), God gives us spiritual gifts — supernaturally charged spices that best accomplish his purposes through us. Those gifts often complement our natural abilities.

> *God weaves into our recipe some very special spices that fit us alone.*

For example, God often uses three of my spiritual gifts — mercy, encouragement, and teaching (Romans 12) — to accompany my natural love for English and writing, especially in greeting cards or books. Those gifts are also the prime "motivators" behind everything I do, whether I'm teaching a Bible study, writing a new book, parenting my kids, or simply listening to a friend.

But discovering our unique, "spicy" gifts may involve a trial-and-error process. Sometimes we women hide behind other women's spices, adapting ourselves to their recipes instead of using our own. Often, we need God's help and others' advice in abandoning our fears, our excuses, and our unfair comparisons. Some of us still have trouble accepting who we really are — truly gifted women who are loved, accepted, and treasured by our heavenly Father.

God often helps us discover our gifts in strange ways. Sometimes he develops our gifts through *pleasure*. What do you enjoy doing? What are your natural abilities? What have you attempted that brought only frustration? What could you do for hours and never know the time was passing? (Sorry, shopping doesn't count here.) What are your strengths?

Sometimes God develops our spices through the pain in our lives. What are your weaknesses? How has God brought good out of painful experiences in your life? A friend of mine realized a life-long dream of becoming a missionary through the pain of divorce when her husband left her. Walking through some difficult marriage issues of our own helped propel my husband and I into a marriage enrichment ministry — and even the writing of a marriage book to help other couples.

But God also chooses to develop our spices through the plain — or ordinary — events of life. While it may not sound glamorous, if you'll pay close attention, you may find God's signature on your life in a number of unlikely places: in the clutter of a noisy kitchen, in the midnight hours of a baby's cuddling, in the hectic pace of your business, or on a mission trip overseas.

The next time you're tempted to deny your giftedness as a woman or think your spice doesn't count, consider your favorite recipe without the needed salt or other spice. If you don't use it, who will benefit from it?

Not you, not others, and certainly not God. Spice up your world for Jesus! You truly can make a difference.

DAY-BREAK

Think about the things you enjoy doing. What activities, events, or organizations have brought you the most pleasure and success? How has God used pain in your life to touch others? How does God use you in the plain moments in life?

DAY-BRIEF

Any spice is nice in the hands of the Master Chef.

DAY-VOTEDLY YOURS

God, I know you have given me gifts with your name on them. Help me use them unselfishly to spice up my world for you.

day 22
when the battle's raging

Aaron and Hur held his hands up — one on one side, one on the other — so that his hands remained steady until sunset.
Exodus 17:12

A Bible teacher of a large men's class, my grandfather knew the Word. Just before he died of leukemia, he made a strange request of the ones standing by his bedside. He asked that someone hold his hands up high over his head. Poppe was too weak from cancer to hold them up by himself. He needed a steadying hand. Death was drawing near. For him, it was a symbol of winning the battle — and crossing over into heaven — from death to life.

His request made sense as I later studied a passage in Exodus. The Israelites' trek through the wilderness included one challenge after another. After the Israelites left Egypt, God used the "hand" of Moses, along with Moses' staff, to usher in God's miracles in the parting of the Red Sea and in the provision of water through a rock at Horeb when the people complained of thirst. God continually used Moses throughout their forty-year journey as a tower of strength to accomplish his purposes and to meet every need of the people.

But Moses also grew tired. When the Amalekites attacked the Israelites at Rephidim, Moses sent his faithful aide Joshua to round up some men for an all-out battle. Moses applied his strength where it would lend the most support. He held up his hands, along with God's staff, to ensure God's blessing for victory. As long as Moses held up his hands with the staff, the Israelites were winning. But when Moses' arms grew heavy and sagged, the scales tipped, and the enemy prevailed.

Moses' brother Aaron and his brother-in-law Hur saw Moses' predicament and climbed the hill to help. Pushing a stone under Moses so he could sit and rest, they then stood on either side and propped up the leaning tower of Moses. Each held up one of Moses' hands until the battle was over and the Israelites conquered their enemies (see Exodus 17).

As women friends and sisters in Christ, we can be the hands that stretch another's faith toward heaven.

Where would we be as women without the helping hand of another to prop us up when we're leaning and losing the war? Whether we're fighting in the thick of the battle or directing it ourselves, there are times when a helping hand can spell the difference between life and death.

You may have stood there in the past, or you may be facing that situation now. Perhaps you know someone else who is trying to survive: a friend who is struggling to find hope again after losing a child or husband; a mother, distraught with her rebellious teen, who is ready to give up; a teenager who is planning to abort her baby unless someone intervenes; a wife who is growing weary of pretending that her husband still loves her; or a single mom of four kids who just received a pink slip at work and has no plan B.

Where will they go? What will they do? To whom will they turn?

All of us, no matter what the personal battle is, will need a helping hand at times. As women friends and sisters in Christ, we can be the hands that stretch another's faith toward heaven. Whatever is in your hand — a staff to help lead the way, a place to sit and rest awhile, comforting words of encouragement to cushion the pain, or a warm hug to steady another's arms — offer it to the one whose battle is raging.

And when we do, God gives us the distinct privilege of helping turn a person's sign of surrender, or giving up — the lifting up of hands toward heaven — into a hope-filled, hand-raising, praise of victory.

DAY-BREAK

Are you fighting any battles right now? Is anyone helping to steady your hands? Whom do you know that needs a helping hand? Will you call or write them today?

DAY-BRIEF

To the one engaged in battle, a helping hand spells H-O-P-E.

DAY-VOTEDLY YOURS

Lord, there are times when the word *battle* makes me want to go "AWOL." But when I realize all the times you steadied my hands and lifted my head, I want to help others as well. Use my hands, my heart, my hugs, my life, Lord, to help someone who is struggling today.

day 23
apples of gold

A word aptly spoken is like apples of gold in settings of silver.
Proverbs 25:11 NIV

"What did you do that for, _____?"

She might as well have completed that statement with her implied meaning: "Stupid!" That's how I interpreted her tone of voice, anyway. And it was not the first time I had been on the receiving end of her barbed statements.

As soon as Larry and I married, I signed up with a temporary work agency, the best choice available for me with my limited experience. I was barely nineteen, could type well, but my only work experience was as a department store clerk selling clothes and keeping sales records during my senior year of high school. With my husband still in college, we couldn't survive on his small pastor's salary and his minimum wage job on the paint crew at the university.

My first assignment took me on a trial basis to an old home, fashioned into a community agency's business office, where I worked for two older women. After a few weeks, they liked my work and decided to hire me full-time as a secretary and bookkeeper.

But I wasn't prepared for the months that would follow. My job also included everything from cleaning up the old kitchen, to sorting through large piles of "donations," to occasionally watering the huge grounds surrounding the old building. Somehow I managed to break an antique pitcher in the kitchen cleanup, and one day accidentally left the water on, flooding the entire yard. When I mistakenly deposited $2,000 in the wrong bank account, the women were sure an expensive audit would follow swiftly — all because of *my* error.

Both women expected equal work time. Yet one would continually wait until an hour before closing and want me to complete four hours of work by five o'clock. They vied for my time and attention like vultures hovering over a fresh kill.

It wasn't so much the imbalanced workload or unreal expectations, but the words and/or lack of them that sent me sprawling across my bed in tears when I returned home on many nights. I know I was young and inexperienced and made some foolish mistakes, but their lack of sensitivity at times left me drained and discouraged. I never complained to them about the work (only to my husband, bless his heart).

Appropriate, carefully chosen words bring joy,
both to the person speaking and to the hearer.

I hadn't yet discovered my love of words and writing at that time, but I knew enough to recognize the power of positive, encouraging words. Appropriate, carefully chosen words bring joy, both to the person speaking and to the hearer. I desperately wanted that to happen. Like stones or cushions, words can either knock us down or make us feel better and more relaxed. I don't have to tell you which metaphor fit my situation.

My work ended after a year. It was a short season, but it was a good learning experience for me. Among other things, it firmed up my belief about the powerful influence and effect of "a word aptly spoken."

Although I would fail many times, I determined early on that with God's help, I would always try to paint word pictures that would bring beauty, encouragement, and healing — ones that would create "apples of gold in settings of silver" in the hearts of others.

Because those are the kind that truly change lives.

DAY-BREAK

How has the power of words affected you negatively? Positively? Is there someone who needs your encouragement today? What can you say that will truly make a difference in someone's life?

DAY-BRIEF

Never underestimate the power of a timely word.

DAY-VOTEDLY YOURS

Lord, your words have filled my heart with beauty and life. Thank you for reminding me often of how much you value me as your child. Use me to bless others and add value to their lives.

reborn

But to all who believed him and accepted him,
he gave the right to become children of God. They are reborn.
John 1:12 – 13 NLT

Childless women, older moms, empty nesters — many of them have bought into the new phenomenon called "reborning." Doll artists who wanted to create truly lifelike collectibles started enhancing vinyl baby dolls, remaking them to look like authentic babies. Eventually, they began creating vinyl kits, and the reborning craze eventually spread. From translucent skin tones, soft baby folds, moveable limbs, and natural dimples and smiles, each doll's features look so real that people literally mistake them for a real baby.[5]

The dolls cost from five hundred to thousands of dollars. That may seem like a lot of money to spend on a doll, especially for a non-collector. But according to an ABC's *20/20* television series, some women buy them for the attention the dolls bring. They dress their lifelike dolls in authentic baby clothes and even stroll or carry them to the store or to a park. And people respond as if the cuddly dolls were real babies. For a barren woman who has no grandmother bragging rights, the doll appeals to the maternal instinct.

A woman who has experienced multiple miscarriages may feel her reborn doll helps her ease some of the emotional pain from her loss. Still others whose nest has emptied believe it's a way of preserving memories of the less traumatic moments of motherhood.

Some professionals call the reborning fad a prop — a substitutionary way of dealing with loss or failure of a parent. But some women who have happy, well-adjusted children of their own love the dolls and even hold birthday parties for them.[6]

Although one vinyl doll may cost five hundred dollars, many women feel the dolls are definitely less expensive than adoption. After all, dolls are forever babies; they never change. No dirty diapers, no hospital bills, no midnight feedings, no school fees, no heartaches, no dating traumas, no college tuition, and no wedding costs. But neither will there be any wet kisses, syrupy hugs, or tiny fingers wrapping around your heart. No heart-to-heart talks and no sharing celebrations.

> *Whether we've raised children or not,*
> *we who have come to know and experience*
> *Christ's love firsthand can use our own "reborning"*
> *experience with God to help meet the needs of others.*

There is obviously a strong, therapeutic value in these extraordinary dolls — and it is a truly remarkable art form. But maybe there's an additional investment women can make — even those who never bore children — to fuel their God-given instincts naturally, and in a way that blesses them — and others.

Thousands upon thousands of children need our touch, our attention, our wisdom, and our love. If money or opportunity won't allow adoption, then maybe we can offer to care for others' kids through foster care, or even try to influence little minds and hearts through church, school, or community programs. Scores of young moms are separated from their mothers by death or distance and long for a nearby support system — often through a mentor, a mother "substitute" to help them through both the midnight crises of their lives and the ordinary, day-to-day challenges we women all experience.

"But I've never had children," someone might say. "How can I possibly help?"

Do you love children? Are you a woman? Simply share your life and your love — the things children need the most.

Whether we've raised children or not, perhaps we who have come to know and experience Christ's love firsthand can use our own "reborning" experience with God to help meet the needs of others. We can share the way God has "remade" us into his special children, and we can pass on the wisdom he has invested in us. And it won't cost us much but time, energy — and a whole bundle of love and caring.

And the rewards last forever.

DAY-BREAK

If you have no children, how would you feel about "adopting" a child of someone you know — in the sense of being available to offer help from time to time? What are some ways you can reach out to the children of your church or community?

DAY-BRIEF

Children offer us a second chance at life.

DAY-VOTEDLY YOURS

Lord Jesus, help us see life — and children — through your eyes, not our own. Thank you that you didn't consider the expense of your life too great a sacrifice to give for your children. Thank you for loving me, even through all of my growing pains.

miracle in the rain

God's voice thunders in marvelous ways;
he does great things beyond our understanding.
He says … to the rain shower, "Be a mighty downpour."
Job 37:5 – 6

God captured Jami's heart for missions when she was only ten years old.

By the time she finished her sophomore year in high school, Jami felt God calling her to India for five weeks, where she combined evangelistic drama with personal evangelism. While there, Jami faced a test of her faith perhaps unlike any she had ever experienced.

Every evening Jami's team would travel from their base village to the distant, outlying places where they would present their evangelistic drama in the remote villages. The villagers worked in their fields during the day, so the drama team's only option was visiting them at night.

While part of the team set up the audio equipment in the particular language of that village, the other team members fanned out in groups, inviting the villagers to follow them to watch their special presentation.

The team's usual method was to first present their drama and then a team member would explain its spiritual meaning, using a translator to convey their message. Then the team would break into small predesignated groups and go out with translators, visiting the people who had seen the drama. Names of those people who responded favorably to the gospel message would be given to the local pastors and missionaries in the area for follow-up and discipleship.

One night Jami's group was preparing to present the drama a second time as darkness fell. Her team was about to disperse and invite more villagers to see the drama when it started to sprinkle. Jami's leaders shouted to her and the team: "Hurry and start the drama! Maybe we can beat the rain!"

They knew once it started raining, their opportunity to share God's message would be next to impossible: the team could make no presentation, and in turn, no people would see it. Likely, none of the villagers would stay and get drenched in the rain.

While the first half of the presentation began, the team members whose parts in the drama weren't until later, including Jami, huddled at the back of the "stage," praying for the people of this village. As they began their petition, Jami said God laid an intense burden on each of the team members for the lost people of the village. Jami explained it best in her own words:

"I'm not talking a normal burden for the lost; I mean, we were all literally crying for the people. A spirit of prayer fell on us and we were all praying out loud at once. The rain continued. We prayed louder and louder and with increasing passion, begging God to intervene: 'God, please stop the rain! God, we want these people to stay so they can know you. PLEASE stop the rain!'"

But as the prayers intensified, so did the rain. Finally, a

torrential downpour drenched not only their bodies, but their spirits as well. The continuing rain spread a sense of anxiety throughout the team. And for a few moments, Jami was frustrated and confused. *What was God up to? Was he listening? Did they not pray with faith? Was something preventing God from saying yes to their prayers? Didn't God know they would give him the glory for his affirmative answer to their prayers? Didn't God want these people to know him? Didn't he want to change their lives?*

When the time came for Jami and some of her team members to present their part in the drama, they turned around, not knowing if they would face an empty audience. But their mouths gaped open in shock. Before them stood a multitude of silent, intense villagers watching with eyes wide open, their hair wet and clothes soaked — and raindrops still pelting their bodies. Not only had the people who had originally come that night stayed through the entire drama, but also many more villagers had slogged through the rain to see the team's presentations.

Sometimes, miracles happen when we least expect them.

Why on earth would these people stand out in the dark and the rain? Why didn't they leave and go home? The team members were witnessing a miracle from Jesus, but they couldn't understand why — or what — was really happening until after they finished the drama.

But Jesus knew what he was doing. When the presentations and follow-ups were completed, the team went out in groups to ask if anyone wanted to follow Jesus right then. That night, over two hundred people in the village accepted Jesus as Lord and Savior.

One of Jami's team members asked an elder in the village after he had accepted Jesus why so many people in his village had responded to the gospel so quickly and yet so firmly. The man looked at him and simply said, "It has not rained in our village for three years ... but when your group came, your God sent rain!"

That experience changed not just the villagers, but the team members as well. Later, Jami reflected on one of the things God taught her: "Sometimes we pray the rain will stop. But sometimes, it's in the rain that miracles happen."

God doesn't always answer the way we expect — or ask. But aren't you glad he doesn't? Faith is trusting God even when we don't understand what he's doing — which is much of the time. And sometimes, miracles happen when we least expect them.

Whether your "rain" is a watery downpour from heaven or a torrent of endless crises, remember God is in control of both. And he has an indisputable track record.

DAY-BREAK

When was the last time you asked God to do something, and he answered a totally different way than you had anticipated? What did you learn from that experience? How did you draw closer to him through it?

DAY-BRIEF

When God is in control, every moment is a miracle.

DAY-VOTEDLY YOURS

God, thank you for the faithful way you answer us — in your own time and in your own way. Strengthen our faith as we learn to trust you more in big and little ways. And especially, today, Lord, thank you for the "rain."

there you are!

*You know … how God anointed Jesus of Nazareth with
the Holy Spirit and power, and how he went around doing good.*
Acts 10:37 – 38

"You have a beautiful smile."

A stranger had clipped my senior picture from the local paper
and enclosed it with a hand-written, encouraging note in the mail.
It was a simple gesture that took maybe five or ten minutes, but did
you guess I started flashing my pearly whites after that?

Years later I remembered that incident and thought, *Maybe I
can help put a smile on others' faces too.* I began to watch our local newspaper for articles about people "in the news." Wedding announce-
ments, death notices, school honorees, feature articles — anything
that warranted a "Good for you!" "Way to go!" "I'm so sorry!" or
"I'm praying for you!" — I cut them out.

Each week I'd grab a note card and pen and write a personal
note that fit the particular honor or occasion in the person or family's life. Occasionally, I'd add, "You have a beautiful smile." I lived
in a smaller town at the time, so finding their addresses in the local
phone book was not too difficult.

Sometimes people would call to express their appreciation —
and probably their curiosity as well. "Why would I, a perfect

stranger, take the time to send them a clipping and note?" Good question.

I assured them I had no ulterior motive. I was simply copying a kind deed done for me when I was a senior in high school. It made me feel special, and I just wanted to return the kindness — like a boomerang — to someone else. Sometimes this small gesture opened the door for an opportunity to share the good news about Jesus. Then I could tell them how really special they were to God too.

> *Someone has said when you give something away*
> *— like time, energy, and encouragement*
> *— you give away life.*

Through the years, sending greeting cards has replaced that particular ministry, but when I look at the life of Jesus, I realize he spent his entire short life on earth "doing good." Everywhere he went, Jesus healed lives, spoke peace, embraced children, taught truth, and encouraged others. If, when you encountered Jesus, you didn't feel "special," it wasn't his fault. Jesus was and is the Savior of the world. Knowing him doesn't always eliminate discomfort, pain, and misunderstanding with others, but Jesus came because he loved people, and he wanted to give life — full and abundant (John 10:10). He restored worth, renewed hope, and refreshed spirits.

Someone has said when you give something away — like energy, time, and encouragement — you give away life. Jesus went a step further. Everything he did was good, but he truly gave away life — through his own lifeblood.

A friend of ours named Al Brown ("Big Al") seemed to have the knack of making others feel special in his own way. He called everyone he met "Boss." People used to wonder why. Al died suddenly at the age of sixty-one. He was laughing one minute, as he often did (kids used to mistake him for Santa Claus in or out of costume) — and the next minute he was gone.

At his funeral, Al's pastor explained: Apparently calling each person "Boss" was how Al let people know they were what mattered most in his presence. Instead of saying, "Here I am!" it was his way of saying, "There you are!" It often opened the door for Al to share about his "real Boss," the Lord Jesus Christ, and what a joy it was living for him.

A smile, a word, a note, a lifestyle — where there's life, there's a way to make someone else special.

What a way to live!

DAY-BREAK

What can you give away this week? How can you make someone feel special? Each time you encounter others this week, practice thinking, "There you are!"

DAY-BRIEF

Focusing on others always improves your outlook.

DAY-VOTEDLY YOURS

Jesus, remind me daily to "do good" wherever I go. Thank you for every opportunity you give to make your name known and to help others feel special.

the upside of down

Though the fig tree does not bud
and there are no grapes on the vines,
though the olive crop fails
and the fields produce no food …
yet I will rejoice in the LORD,
I will be joyful in God my Savior.

Habakkuk 3:17 – 18

One year my husband returned from an overseas mission trip to Europe. His team visited Romania in the months following the fall of Communism. Larry always brings me a small gift when he travels, but this time he apologized for coming home empty-handed.

He told me about finding empty shops and grocery stores, sometimes with only one loaf of bread or a handful of assorted canned goods on the shelves. Once fertile farmland lay barren, stripped of its nutrients through neglect and chemical abuse. The corrupt dictatorship had literally wasted the land, and the people were suffering the consequences.

Fortunately, the change of leadership has brought some measure of improvement to the daily lives of people, but many former Eastern bloc countries still live in poverty. Give them money and a choice of how to use it, and the majority will probably spend it on survival — milk, water, food for their children, and medicine for their families.

At the writing of this devotion, America is going through an economic crisis. It is not like the Great Depression of 1929 that our parents, grandparents, or great-grandparents survived, but for some, it's still a nightmare from which they have not awakened. Is there any bright side to these times?

For women, and for all of us living in the United States or comparably "wealthy" nations, is there any message God would like for us to "get"? Am I trying to put a guilt trip on those who live wealthy lifestyles? Absolutely not.

> *Hard times can be a spiritual wake-up call*
> *that something is desperately wrong*
> *and in need of fixing.*

When financial crises occur — and they probably will come to all of us at one time or another — we have the opportunity to rethink the priorities of our lives. When we see the Dow plunging, it's a catch – 22 scenario. We need more jobs to provide for the inevitable losses, and that means more "goods" for people to select. And people must have money to "buy" necessities, yes — but they'll also purchase stuff they don't need, in order to rev up the banks' lending power for things like nice homes, cars, new businesses — "basic" things America depends on, but which many people never possess.

Greed has the potential of both paralyzing and petrifying human hearts. Life in a materialistic culture has so complicated the economy that most of us can't visualize any simple solutions. But somewhere, a still, small voice — no, a holy Creator's voice — still whispers to us: "I will always meet your needs. Read my lips in the pages of Scripture. Seek first my kingdom. Obey me in all things. Claim my promises. Learn my truths. Live unselfishly. Give generously. Live honestly. Walk justly. Know me. And make my ways known. Trust me ... Trust me ... Trust me."

Is that the answer to prosperity? That depends on what you call "prosperity." It *is* the answer to life and real living. Hard times can be a spiritual wake-up call that something is desperately wrong and in need of fixing. It may be a time of reevaluation and reaffirming of gratitude for what we do have. But for us as women, it is also an opportunity to draw near to and celebrate the heart of a faithful God, regardless of what is happening in our lives.

God is waiting for women who will give more, spend less, love deeply, forgive freely, see clearly, believe boldly, serve joyfully, act wisely, and trust God completely.

Will that help our economy? Maybe, maybe not. But it will transform your life and usher you into another realm that many cannot comprehend.

And one by one, it can transform the hearts of others.

DAY-BREAK

Have you ever endured a financial crisis? What did God teach you through that experience? If you have never done so, begin a "gratitude" journal or a "blessing catcher," and ask God to help you fill it daily with reminders of his goodness and grace.

DAY-BRIEF

No relationship can prosper without trust.

DAY-VOTEDLY YOURS

Father, you are the one constant in my life. No matter what happens, I choose to trust you deeply and to seek a more intimate walk with you daily. Thank you for teaching me that in the good times and in the bad, you are always there.

day 28

awestruck

When Simon Peter saw this, he fell at Jesus' knees and said,
"Go away from me, Lord; I am a sinful man!"
Luke 5:8

Fishing 101: *Fish in the early morning or evening.* That's when the fish usually bite. That rule is to inform those of you women who have never cast a net — or line — into the watery deep. At least that's what my grandfather, father, and husband taught me through the years. I've never won any trophies, but I have caught my share of keepers: a couple of six-pounders and a near seven. (But you should have seen the ones that got away.) I do love to fish with my husband.

But rules are sometimes broken, and fish occasionally bite at noon in the heat of the day. At least they did for Peter, James, and John. Except they didn't exactly, um, "bite."

Peter, James, and John had fished all night and caught nothing. Observing them clean their nets, Jesus climbed into one of the nearby boats and began to teach the people who had crowded around the shore to hear him. When he finished, he told Peter to go into deep water and let down the nets again.

Peter objected, but then obeyed. Guess what! Good fishing hole! The school of fish swarming into their net was so large that even with an additional boat to help, the vessels nearly sank from the load. Immediately, Peter recognized this man as being different, completely other than him. Compared to Jesus, Peter called himself a sinful man and fell at Jesus' feet (Luke 5:1–9).

On numerous occasions in Scripture, those who encountered divinity exclaimed essentially the same thing. Moses removed his sandals (Exodus 3:5). Isaiah cried, "Woe to me!... I am a man of unclean lips" (Isaiah 6:5). And John, in his heavenly vision, "fell at his feet as though dead" (Revelation 1:17). Each in his own way expressed a deep reverence for a holy God.

> *God's blessings should bring the same awestruck awareness of a holy, awesome God as if we were "seeing" him through a supernatural revelation — that "other than us" feeling.*

But most responded that way because they had encountered someone or something unknown to them — a fearful, awesome, mind-boggling image of God and his character. Peter too expressed fear. But here, his reaction stems from the blessing God gave. Catching a multitude of fish in the middle of the day was truly a miracle. Ordinary stuff for Jesus, but extraordinary to Peter. And in Peter's case, God used what happened as a visual illustration of what he wanted to do in Peter's life: "From now on you will fish for people" (Luke 5:10).

We may never encounter an experience like Moses, Isaiah, or John, but God sends blessings our way every day. I like to call the really special ones "God-things." But in reality, all of his blessings are "God-things." How do we respond? How many women cry, "Lord, get away from me, for I am a sinful woman!" at their wedding celebration, at the birth of their children, on the receipt of their college diploma, or at the landing of a fabulous job?

What am I saying? That God's blessings should bring the same awestruck awareness of a holy, awesome God as if we were "seeing" him through a supernatural revelation — that "other than us" feeling. It's not a negative, guilty declaration but a grateful, honest estimation of who we really are in contrast to who God really is. And Peter recognized it immediately. But Jesus didn't want to "get away" from Peter. He wanted to draw Peter into his net of followers. He wants that for all of us.

The next time God blesses you, think about your response. Whether *you* call it a miracle or not doesn't matter. Every miracle is an awesome act of God. And every act of God *is* a divine miracle. It can't be explained away or credited to humanity. If anything, those "God-things" only underline the extreme difference between the two — the divine and the human.

And every time God blesses you, it is an opportunity to "go fishing" and tell someone about what he has done.

DAY-BREAK

When was the last time you recognized one of God's blessings as a divine miracle? How will you respond the next time God blesses you?

DAY-BRIEF

Your availability always affects your ability.

DAY-VOTEDLY YOURS

Lord Jesus, when I think of how many times you have blessed me throughout my life, I fall on my knees in wonder — and gratitude. How great you are! Lord, I will be a follower and a fisherwoman for you. Keep filling my nets so I have plenty to give away.

replaced, but not erased

Forget the former things;
> *do not dwell on the past.*
See, I am doing a new thing!
> *Now it springs up; do you not perceive it?*
Isaiah 43:18 – 19

In the blink of an eye, the "presidential" website changed. As soon as the new president, Barack Obama, completed his vows — the presidential oath — that would officially make him America's newest leader, a new screen appeared. Like an Etch-a-Sketch®, the pictures, words, and position of former President George Bush were erased and replaced by images of the new president. Out with the old, in with the new.

As I watched the former president and his wife board the helicopter to take them away, I wondered what kind of emotions hovered near the surface as they waved good-bye.

It was a usual and necessary transition, yet in this technological age, the visual replacement on the website seemed to highlight the reality — and the symbolism.

I know women who have experienced a similar "replacement." No, not as a president of a country, but in their role as a wife, one of

God's most honorable positions. For some, the emotions flooded in as they heard the words, "I don't love you anymore"; "I met someone else"; or "I'm leaving you." And before they could even blink an eye, it seemed, a sacred union between a man and a woman was erased — replaced by another. Many of them stood by helplessly, waving good-bye, with emotions brimming near the surface.

What do you say to a woman whose life has just been ripped apart and replaced by someone younger, someone more attractive, or maybe even her best friend? And with no apparent good reason or prior warning, the pain deepens even more. A president's "vows" last only a maximum of eight years in his position as president. But a marriage? The vows make it clear: "until death do us part."

He is the God of new beginnings.

Divorce can seem like a death for the one who has been replaced. There is no helicopter standing by, no welcome reception waiting, no mansion or "new life" to anticipate.

Maybe you've been there and done that, or you know someone who has. In our fallen world filled with selfish humanity, the statistics don't lie. "Replacement" is a word that cuts into the heart of Christian women too.

God intends for vows to be kept — and you honored yours. But if you are the one still flinching from the sting of being replaced, hear me — or rather hear God's words to you. You may feel like the people of Israel who thought God had put up a new website: "The LORD has forsaken me, the Lord has forgotten me" (Isaiah

49:14). He even had good reason to erase them, because of their grievous sin and idolatry. They had left him and broken their vows to him. Yet God kept his promise to Israel. They would always be his people. "I will not forget you!" he assured them (Isaiah 49:15).

And he will do the same for you. Whether you are the "replacer," the "replacement," or the one being replaced — God will not "erase" you. He is constantly thinking of you. He will not forget about sin and its natural consequences, because he is a righteous, holy God. But he will forgive those who truly seek him — even those who have hurt you.

God has a big picture in mind. If you are a child of God, you have entered into a holy union. He wants none to perish. He wants only to restore, not to replace. He still has a plan for your life. He is the God of new beginnings.

One day, in the blinking of an eye, Jesus will return for his bride. At that moment, you will forget the pain of being replaced forever. A host of angels will escort you to your waiting room in heaven. As a flurry of joyful emotions spill over, you will suddenly realize: you are home, and you will never have to wave good-bye again (1 Thessalonians 4:16 – 17).

DAY-BREAK

Have you or someone you know been through a divorce? How can you encourage them this week? If that someone is you, start a journal. Write down the emotions you are experiencing, and as you read Scripture, record any promises you find.

DAY-BRIEF

God wants to erase sin, not people.

DAY-VOTEDLY YOURS

Father, I know you are the God of new beginnings, and I'm asking you to start a new work in me. Replace my fears and disappointments with the joy of your sweet presence. I need you!

three times a winner

Hope deferred makes the heart sick,
but a longing fulfilled is a tree of life.
Proverbs 13:12

Cancer is not something you wish on anyone — not once, not twice — and of course not *three* times. Is it "Three strikes, you're out!" or "Third time is the charm"? Michelle Blackshear chooses the second one.

When she was twenty-two years old, Michelle was studying occupational therapy at Texas Woman's University in Denton, Texas. One day her neck seemed stiff, and her fingers felt a lump above her collarbone. The diagnosis? Hodgkin's lymphoma. After abdominal staging surgery, doctors determined she "only" had to have radiation to beat it.

In May 1990, Michelle's cancer was pronounced in remission. So she went on with life. She continued with college, married a wonderful husband in 1991, and gave birth to their son in 1993.

The year 2000 turned out to be memorable, but not because it was the turn of the century. After three months of being misdiagnosed with the flu, Michelle received the verdict of Acute Myelogenous Leukemia (AML). That entailed the entire months of September and November inside the hospital, with the month of October at home resting. Chemotherapy was horrendous, to say the least.

September 2007 marked seven years in remission for Michelle. It also meant the big 4 – 0 for her, which required yearly mammograms from then on. But after her checkup, she was called back for more views because of some "suspicious" spots. More mammograms, sonograms, and biopsies — only to find out she had breast cancer! Because of the radiation that cured her Hodgkin's disease, she was at a great risk for this. But Michelle didn't think it would happen so soon. And so her journey began, again. Surgery followed, but the good news is, as of November 2008, she is now cancer free!

Michele loves life, so she wasted no time moving forward. "Not having my degree has bugged me for a very long time. I had given up that dream several years ago, but now I know that it just wasn't my time. I think God must look at me sometimes and think, 'Girl, I know what I am doing — have you forgotten that *again?*' If for some reason it doesn't happen, I am okay with that as long as I am giving it a try."

God is not only the dream-maker;
he is the dream-fulfiller.

From her blog, Michelle recorded her thoughts about her first day back in college: "A beautiful clear and sunny day … Two of my favorite songs on the radio … I am home now, and I am crying. Why? Because this is a HUGE day for me — I went back to college for the first time in sixteen years! It is H-U-G-E.

"I am not sad; I am overcome with emotion because I never thought I could do this, until just a few months ago! I AM GOING TO FINISH MY DEGREE! I think I am overwhelmed because it is the first really normal thing I have done in so many years that is not a compromise! I am doing something I have always desired — for me. I'm not being a volunteer to help a school or function; I am not being a substitute teacher — because it is my only qualification. I will not be sitting here this time next year, wondering what I had accomplished the year before. This time ... I am doing something for myself, to be a better me! I am just overwhelmed how completely obvious God has been in this! Today ... I am weepy, but not at all sad. Just being emotional me!"[7]

Does God care about the dreams and desires of a woman? Yes! Like Michelle, you may have faced insurmountable odds. Life has no certainty. But we have Jesus. "In him, we live and move and have our being" (Acts 17:28).

Like cancer, hope may lie dormant for years, buried under a pile of dirty laundry or a mountain of bills. It may surface occasionally, only to hide again within the folds of stress, worry, and sickness. But when the time is right, and only God knows when, he will fulfill that longing of yours. Like a tiny, divine seed planted in the fertile soil of your heart, that God-given desire will spring up and begin to grow and blossom.

Women are by nature givers and nurturers. That's a tiring work. Often your needs and desires may seem selfish to you. But God loves to nurture *you*! He is not only the dream-maker; he is the dream-fulfiller.

If for some reason, as Michelle indicated above, we never reach our dreams in their totality, the God of hope has also nestled another truth deep in our spirits, so that with the psalmist, we can cry out sincerely to him, "Whom have I in heaven but you? And earth has nothing I desire besides you" (Psalm 73:25).

With that kind of confession, we're always a winner!

DAY-BREAK

What dreams has God given to you? What obstacles have you overcome to be where you are today? Write down at least one God-given dream in your heart not yet realized, and commit it to God today.

DAY-BRIEF

A dream is a window of hope God wants to open for all of his children.

DAY-VOTEDLY YOURS

God, thank you for the dreams you have placed within my heart — the ones already fulfilled and others still waiting in line. Grant me the wisdom to know which desires are from you. More than anything else, you are my heart's desire, Lord!

day 31
the stuff of life

Martha, Martha ... you are worried and upset about many things,
but few things are needed — or indeed only one. Mary has chosen
what is better, and it will not be taken away from her.
Luke 10:41 – 42

Most women are familiar with Jesus' challenge to Martha's priorities and his words, "Mary has chosen what is better." Some might
think Jesus was asking Martha to change her personality: "Martha,
you need to be like Mary" — the one more reflective and quiet, who
seemed to hang on Jesus' every word as she sat at his feet that day
in their home.

But those who understand his true meaning know Jesus was
simply asking Martha to alter her choice of priorities. Food for the
body was necessary, and generous hospitality was a *good* choice, but
not at the expense of forgetting her reasons for serving Jesus in the
first place. Even with her own personality, Jesus wanted Martha to
make the better choice: to seek him first and eliminate unnecessary distractions that would steal her devotion from him (Luke
10:38 – 41).

But what if you hear Jesus whisper to you, "You need to be a
Martha" for a while? No, not in the sense of becoming a fussy host-
ess. Somehow, I also pictured Martha as an organized, meticulous
woman. There was a time — it's foggy in my memory — when I

might have morphed into a "Martha," even if just for a day. When company was coming, I'd shift gears and go on a cleaning binge. But no more. Okay, maybe Jesus didn't say those exact words — "Be a Martha" — but that's what I *heard* in my spirit. Let me explain.

One of the things my husband and I have, um, "discussed" the most in our marriage is "stuff," or where to put our stuff, or how to get rid of stuff. I've argued that, compared to *most* women, my accumulation of stuff is small. Besides, I add, "I'm a 'Mary,' not a Martha. It's in my genes. And creative minds don't have time to deal with these kinds of issues." He argues that it's not how much we *have*, but how much will fit into the house, not the garage or attic.

> *Only God can help us women to do*
> *the impossible things that our nature, our time,*
> *or our stubborn wills can't seem to accomplish.*

Perhaps it was a long-time promise to my husband that pushed me into a major disposal kick three years ago. That "God-whisper" was so loud I even told the Lord, "If it means giving up writing, I am going to do this for my husband." And I meant it. If I had known it would consume almost two years of my life, perhaps I would not have uttered my vow so hastily. It meant shutting down what I loved to do the most. Of course, I did have a little motivational help. Larry agreed to let me do a little "redecorating" at the same time. That helped to satisfy my creative urges.

We had been through this process on a smaller scale each time we moved, but this was different. I sorted through every drawer, closet, cabinet, and corner. At times, the process was like pulling wisdom teeth. How could I practically give away the huge pine dining table for twelve, the one still carrying the pencil scars from our children's homework, or the rocker that held my babies and me in so many predawn hours? How could I part with the antique icebox — one of the treasures I had picked up for almost pennies years ago? What price tag can you put on memories? Of course, these treasures all sat languishing in the garage, but that was beside the point.

There were tense moments, but we finally worked out a system. I would discard, if Larry would reorganize. I tried to preserve "Mary" moments and priorities, but the writing doors remained for the most part closed. When we finished, the house looked almost new, and I felt "renewed" myself.

I love what God sometimes gives back if we will just say, "I surrender it, Lord. Whether you return it or not is okay." Remember my willingness to give up writing? On the heels of that Martha experience, this devotional is part of that writing, one of a three-book women's series that God *returned* to me — one of those God-things I mentioned in an earlier devotion — and truly only something *he* could do, not me.

Only God can help us do the impossible things that our nature, our time, or our stubborn wills can't seem to accomplish. Some priorities may shift temporarily, depending on our stage of life — or on gentle nudges from his Spirit. But one focus remains the same. Whether our personality fits Mary or Martha doesn't matter. Only one thing truly is needful. As we seek him with an undivided heart, we can complete whatever he asks of us with *his* priorities intact.

That's when all things are truly possible.

DAY-BREAK

How would you describe your personality — as a Mary or a Martha? Why? What kind of changes do you need to make in your life so that you will select "what is better"?

DAY-BRIEF

What you choose is determined by what is in your heart.

DAY-VOTEDLY YOURS

Lord Jesus, I willingly abandon my excuses and my agendas. I'm listening. Teach me your ways and show me your priorities. Above all, I choose you, Lord.

day 32
passion or obsession?

For to me, to live is Christ.
Philippians 1:21

Most of us know the difference between a hobby and an obsession. A hobby is usually something intended for pleasure, an escape, and is usually relegated to leisure time — if we women have any such thing. Painting, reading, scrapbooking, collecting — these are just a few of the ordinary pursuits some women enjoy as a hobby. And most would agree they are fairly passionate or zealous about their interests. In other words, they truly enjoy what they do and work hard to carve out time for it.

But does a hobby ever cross the line? When does a simple, passionate activity turn into a compulsive obsession? If a woman likes art for leisure but fills every space on her wall with her personal creations, and if she spends every spare moment of her day painting to the exclusion of her other responsibilities, we might question what she labels a hobby.

No matter how noble or rewarding, even a woman's work can lead to compulsive activity. She may feel passionate about what she does, whether at home or outside the home. She might even classify it as "God's work." But if she is so driven that she neglects her marriage, her children, and her health, her passion has turned into obsession. When she crosses that invisible boundary — and she usually knows when that happens — there's usually no escape without God's divine help.

God saw that happening with a man named Saul. He was a religious man, and we could easily call his work a passion. But his "zealous" activity drew God's intervention. This thirty-something Pharisee was a sick pursuer of potential prisoners. He lived and breathed threats to persecute new believers in the Christian faith known as "The Way" (Acts 9:1). He was definitely obsessed. That is, until God stepped in.

Passion and obsession aren't always opposites.

While in pursuit of his passionate obsession, Saul experienced a dramatic wake-up call from the Lord himself. A light from heaven blinded him, and the voice of Jesus — whom Saul obviously believed was dead and not resurrected — pointed out Saul's misplaced passion. Jesus explained that Saul was actually persecuting him (see Acts 9:1 – 17).

Saul's life and passion changed that day. And in the months and years to follow, he proved that passion and obsession aren't always opposites. It all depends on the object of your pursuit. Saul, later known to us as Paul, changed his pursuit from persecuting Christians to pursuing God. Enduring prison, shipwreck, hunger, loss, misunderstanding, rejection, and pain never slowed him down. He was both possessed and obsessed by the One who changed his life completely. Paul summarized his passion well: "To me, to live is Christ."

Behind every passion and activity there must be a sense of

balance for us women. Living life fully, loving others sincerely, and pursuing Christ passionately will keep us on track.

What should drive every activity, every passion, and every pursuit of ours is our relationship with Jesus Christ. Steven Curtis Chapman named this passion appropriately in one of his song titles, "Magnificent Obsession."

When we are truly pursuing God, and Jesus is our magnificent obsession, he brings the needed beauty and balance to our lives that we women so long for and need. Only then do passion and obsession truly become equal partners.

DAY-BREAK

What are your hobbies? How much time do you spend pursuing them? What about your work? Does it drive you or draw you closer to God? How would you describe your relationship with Christ? As a hobby, an occasional passion, or a "magnificent obsession"?

DAY-BRIEF

You can possess a passion, but an obsession possesses you.

DAY-VOTEDLY YOURS

Jesus, help me keep my life balanced in my pursuits and passions. Thank you for the ways you pursue me to get my attention at times. Truly, I want you to be my magnificent obsession.

day 33

name your manna

When the Israelites saw it, they said to each other, "What is it?"
Exodus 16:15

Their feet hurt, their stomachs growled, and their faces reflected both frowns and the gritty residue from the sandy terrain of the Desert of Sin. Two and a half months into their wilderness journey after crossing the Red Sea, the Israelites did the one thing common to most of us in such circumstances: they grumbled. "Oh, woe is us! We should have stayed in Egypt. There we could sit around the pots of meat and eat to our heart's content. At least there we could die with full stomachs!" (see Exodus 16:3).

The Israelites didn't *ask* for God's provision; they just *complained* about the lack of what they once had. But God never wavered, even in the midst of an ungrateful mob. In addition to meat — the quail he sent — God provided them rain (Exodus 16:13). But this was a special kind of rain. They called it "manna," what we might label as angel food, or bread from heaven. Their "daily bread" was a white, sticky substance that looked like frost but tasted like honey. It was to be a symbol of trust in a God who could and would provide for his people. But it obviously wasn't what they were expecting.

The Israelites could identify the meat God sent, but they had never seen this white stuff, so they asked, "What is it?" In fact, the word they used to name that waferlike substance, *manna*, literally meant, "What is it?" Later, they grumbled again — this time, because they were bored with their manna recipes (Numbers 11:6). In fact, it didn't take much to set off a new set of whines.

We women have our moments too. Stretched thin by wandering in our semi-desert of womanhood, hungry for change and a speck of sanity, we can complain with the best of them. From remote-control husbands to cranky children, from shrinking bank accounts to aching bodies, we know how to gripe and groan. And God hears them all — these cries from a woman's heart.

He gives us "daily bread," and we may recognize part of his provision. But what about the other things he "rains" down on us? We may visualize one thing; God has another in mind.

> *We can't expect mountain-moving faith if we can't*
> *even trust God to push away the pebbles.*

Obviously the desert heat had skewed the Israelites' memories. "Pots" of meat did not exactly translate into royal fare. And how could they have so quickly forgotten their miraculous passage through the Red Sea? But God knew exactly what his people needed. They were still like babies in their faith, and their trust quotient needed improvement. We can't expect mountain-moving faith if we can't even trust God to push away the pebbles. God wanted a people who would obey him, depend on him alone, and gratefully trust him for *every* provision. How would they acknowledge God later in the "land of milk and honey" if they couldn't even trust him and be grateful for simple, daily bread in the wilderness?

In times of plenty or poverty, we have no right to complain. There are moments in our lives when we need to simply cry out to God, "Give us each day our daily bread," our daily manna — our "what is it?" And then be content with "whatever it is," trusting God that he knows best.

Our God knows where we are and what will ultimately draw us closer to him and make us reflect his image more. He "richly blesses all who call on him" (Romans 10:12), and he has promised to "meet all [our] needs according to the riches of his glory in Christ Jesus" (Philippians 4:19). But when or how he does that is up to him. What we tag as a problem, God may see as an opportunity to trust him. But he wants us to ask, not complain (Luke 11:3).

Don't worry. God has a plan — and he knows what he's doing. However God answers, it's okay to give your "manna" a name — as long as you call it a "blessing."

DAY-BREAK

Where are you in your Christian journey right now? In the "wilderness"? At the beginning, middle, or end? Take time today to list at least three "manna loaves" God has provided for you this week. Then thank him for your daily bread.

DAY-BRIEF

God loves to hear his children say, "Thank you!"

DAY-VOTEDLY YOURS

Father, turn every complaint into a prayer of gratitude. Help me trust you through the wilderness as well as in the "land of milk and honey." You have my best interests at heart, and I long to make my heart solely a place for your interests.

day 34
open hearts, open homes

The Lord opened her heart to respond to Paul's message.
When she and the members of her household were baptized,
she invited us to her home.
Acts 16:14 – 15

"I haven't cleaned house in weeks!" "I'm too busy!" "No time to cook!" "My house is too small!" "I can't afford to entertain!"

Most of us have rationalized our lack of hospitality with at least one of those excuses at one time or another. I have. Multiplied obligations with careers, family, community, and church leave little room for entertaining.

But not for Lydia. A busy professional and seller of purple cloth, she was praying with other women by the river outside the city gate of Philippi when Paul found her. Lydia was a religious woman already, but she had no exposure to the good news of Jesus. When Paul explained the gospel to the women, Lydia became the first convert to Christianity in Macedonia. Following her baptism, she immediately invited Paul and his companions to her home.

Notice the transition: God opened Lydia's heart; then *she* opened her home. No excuses, no reason for delay. You may argue, "But she was probably single — maybe an older woman with no kids, no mess, and hospitality was 'in' then, especially in biblical times. That was customary."

Lydia's age, status, or tradition could have some bearing on her situation. But she was still a busy professional who found time to learn and pray with other women. And she had apparently never met these new itinerant missionaries before that day.

True, there's more than one way to show hospitality. Through simple acts of kindness in our everyday walk of life, we embrace others with God's love. But God touched Lydia's heart — *and* her home. Something extraordinary happened to her that day. Later, after Paul and Silas spent a miraculous night in prison and were released, guess where they found a place of rest and renewal? In Lydia's house. Not only that, *other* believers now gathered there in her home as well (Acts 16:25 – 40). What made them move from the river into Lydia's home?

When Jesus truly touches our hearts, nothing is off limits.

When Jesus truly touches our hearts, nothing is off limits. Our home represents the intimate center of our lives, a prepared place for the presence of Christ to live. Why would we say to him, "You can live here in my heart," and then leave him standing on the doorstep of our homes?

Think about Jesus' hospitality. His arms were always open. Anyone that wanted to could see "Welcome" on the front door of his heart. Jesus had no roof over his head, no place to call his own, yet he knew how to create mansions out of tents. He always welcomed good conversation, and he was far more concerned with a clean heart than a clean house. Before Jesus' death and resurrection, he comforted his disciples with these words about our heavenly homes: "My Father's house has plenty of room; if that were not so, would I have told you that I am going there to prepare a place for you?" (John 14:2).

The size of our home doesn't matter, but the size of our heart does. It's not how unique a meal we can prepare or how brightly the floors shine. Clothes may lie in piles, while towels hang in disarray. Sandwiches can appear on paper plates, while noisy kids run through the halls, but who cares? The truth is, when God opens your heart, he wants a welcome mat on your front porch too.

Our only necessary preparation may simply be to say, "My heart and home belong to you, Lord." You'll soon discover that when you open your heart and home to another, you welcome the Savior as well.

DAY-BREAK

When was the last time you opened your heart and home to others? If it's been too long, what are your excuses? Plan for a time soon when you can make your home available to others for a Bible study, a simple meal, a cup of coffee, or even a short visit.

DAY-BRIEF

A reason can simply be an excuse for not doing the right thing.

DAY-VOTEDLY YOURS

Lord Jesus, forgive me for the times when I place my comfort and schedule before your agenda. Help me to prepare a place in my heart — and in my home — for others.

day 35
share his love

But we have this treasure in jars of clay to show that this
all-surpassing power is from God and not from us.
2 Corinthians 4:7

After my father died, my mom told me about an experience just two weeks prior to his death. They were both browsing at a garage sale, and even in my minister father's weakened condition, he couldn't pass up the opportunity to talk about Jesus. He asked the owner about his spiritual life and encouraged him to choose Jesus.

Hearing that story inspired me to be more proactive in my faith. God gave me an opportunity to do that a few months after Daddy's funeral.

While living in a small rural community for a short time, I met two young teenagers outside one day and decided to take a pie over and meet the rest of their family. The mom was not there, but a few days later, the girls returned my pie plate with a big thank you. I invited them in and offered them some cookies from my clay cookie jar.

In the course of our conversation I asked them about their relationship with Jesus. One said she knew something about that from when she was a child years ago. But the other had no idea what I was talking about. I shared my testimony and explained as best I could how they could come to know Jesus Christ personally, how much he loved them and died for them and wanted to live in their hearts and lives. Before they left, I gave them a tract and encouraged them to pray about what we had discussed.

The following Friday was my birthday. I heard a knock at the door, and there stood the two girls. "May we borrow your lawn mower?" Theirs had broken down.

We headed for the garage to get the mower, but just as I was pulling it out, God's Spirit nudged me with a "now." I asked the girls if they had considered our conversation the other day. They both nodded. "Is there any reason why you couldn't ask Jesus into your heart right now?"

"No," they both replied in unison. I explained again what it meant to be a follower of Jesus. I kept clarifying and asking questions to make sure they understood. Every time, they answered affirmatively.

> **God has entrusted to us a precious treasure:**
> **the message of Jesus that can change a life forever.**

So in the middle of a sweltering July afternoon in our garage, two young women were born into God's kingdom. What a great birthday gift! I hugged them both and told them good-bye. Within two hours, they returned the mower. A few minutes later they left to accompany their father, a truck driver, on one of his trips. By the time they returned, I knew we would probably be moved into town.

But I didn't want to lose touch with them. So a couple of months later, I drove back to the rural community and knocked on their door. I wanted to give the girls some Bible study material to help in their Christian growth. This time their mom was home.

As we began to talk, it was obvious that the girls had not discussed their decision with their mom. I could tell she was offended by what I had shared with the girls, because she asked me, "What was it you saw in my home that made you think God was not here?"

"Oh, n-no!" I stammered. "I saw nothing like that. You see, when my father died recently, I renewed my own commitment to share the love of Jesus with everyone I can. I don't assume anything."

After a few moments of conversation, the mom softened. We concluded a short visit, and I left knowing I might never see the girls again. I kept praying for them as the months and years passed.

Several years later, my husband and I were visiting a lady across town that had visited our church. Soon after we arrived, an older teen walked through the living room. Larry and I both did a double take and looked at each other. "Is that ...?"

Before we could complete our question, the woman introduced her niece to us. She had come to live with her a few months earlier. The teenager was one of the sisters who had made a commitment for Christ in our garage. We hugged again and discovered she had become a strong believer and active in her church youth group.

As we drove away that night, I knew my fathers — my heavenly One and my earthly one — were probably both smiling.

As women, we are only clay vessels, but God has entrusted to us a precious treasure: the message of Jesus that can change a life forever. Whether it's in a garage or a grand palace, others need that treasure.

Only God's Spirit can draw others to himself. But when we make ourselves — and that precious treasure of his love — available, others will truly know it was God's doing, not ours.

DAY-BREAK

How have you made his "treasure" available lately? Ask God to use you as a vessel this week to share his love with someone who needs to hear.

DAY-BRIEF

The more we share his treasure, the more valuable it becomes.

DAY-VOTEDLY YOURS

Lord, thank you for using me, a clay vessel, to hold the special treasure of your love. Open doors this week and show me those who are ready to hear about you.

day 36
invisible wings

Do not forget to show hospitality to strangers,
for by so doing some people have shown hospitality
to angels without knowing it.
Hebrews 13:2

Several years ago we started a Saturday night worship service to ease the crowding on Sunday mornings. One cold night a young man showed up after the service was over. Dressed in a military jacket with a stocking cap pulled down on his head, he stood out from the East Texas congregation. He asked my husband if there was any music going on. Larry told him the music portion had finished, but he invited him to come back the next morning for the regular Sunday morning worship, where we would again have music.

During the course of the conversation, Larry asked him a few questions. "What's your name?"

"Oh, I have many names."

"Where are you from?"

"Oh, everywhere."

"Where are you headed?"

"Nowhere in particular."

"Do you always go to church when you travel?"

"Oh, yes, I'm in church every day."

He left out the door, and in a few minutes Larry looked outside to see where he was going. But he was nowhere in sight. On the way home Larry saw the traveler on the road and pulled up beside the man.

"Can we put you up somewhere for the night?"

"No, I'll be fine."

The man's responses seemed strange in light of most travelers who "visited" our church. Located on a busy state highway, our church was like a beacon to the down and out. Those needing assistance showed up frequently. And they all shared one common denominator: they all asked for some kind of help.

The next morning the traveler appeared again and attended both Sunday morning services. One of our women invited him to a mixed Bible study, which he also attended. After church the man started walking down the road again. On the way home, Larry saw him again and offered to take him to the interstate, not far away. Once again, he engaged the man in conversation.

All around us there are angels "unaware"
— special friends in specific places
who fill our lives with love and care.

"May I buy you something to eat?"

"Oh, I don't eat."

Larry asked the man about his relationship with the Lord.

"Oh, yes, I know him well."

In sharing his faith with the man, Larry got to the part about "sin."

"Oh, I don't sin."

My husband took the man as far as the interstate and let him out.

"Are you sure there's not something we can do for you?"

"No, really. Thanks, I'll be fine."

When Larry came home, he had a puzzled look on his face and began to review the strange events: "Most people have an agenda. They need food, a place to stay, gas money, or a bill to be paid. We do what we can on our limited resources, but some don't like what we offer and walk away. Others complain and grumble, but take what they can get. A few have predictable, fabricated stories. And many are genuinely needy and grateful. But this weekend, I met a man who needed nothing and asked for nothing."

We both looked at each other. I knew what he was about to say.

"Is it possible I just saw an angel?" Larry asked.

We can only scratch our heads and wonder, but all things are possible. Truth *is* stranger than fiction. If God opened our spiritual eyes and the real truth were known, we would see them all around us — these messengers of his who move at his command: sometimes "testing," sometimes helping, sometimes fighting, and sometimes watching and waiting for God's next assignment.

In a world where violence and danger stalk daily, it's refreshing to know that kindness never goes out of style. It isn't necessary for you — or us — to know whether we are encountering angels.

Whether we believe in them or not, these heavenly beings respond to a higher authority and are committed to our safety and welfare, regardless of our blindness.

All around us are angels "unaware" — special friends in specific places, who fill our lives with love and care. And though we may never recognize them as such, nor fully understand their actions, these ambassadors of goodwill leave our hearts warmed forever.

And sometimes, God gives us as women invisible "wings" to practice, not "random kindness," but intentional good. When that happens, we are the blessed ones, not them.

DAY-BREAK

Have you ever encountered an angel unaware? What was the result of that experience? Ask God to help you impact another's life this week with intentional, "angelic" love and kindness.

DAY-BRIEF

You don't have to wear wings to bear the name "angel."

DAY-VOTEDLY YOURS

Heavenly Father, thank you for your messengers daily that move on our behalf and at your command. And thank you for letting me have a part in the angelic work of your kingdom too, just by touching others, one life at a time.

day 37

life is precious

For you created my inmost being;
you knit me together in my mother's womb.
Psalm 139:13

"On May 28, 2002, our doctor delivered the shocking news: our third child, our youngest son, would be born with spina bifida. We didn't even know what those words meant. Someone escorted us to another room where a 'genetic' counselor advised us. The first words out of her mouth were, 'You know this makes it possible for you to have an abortion.'"

Those words touched an intense, angry chord in Dr. Timothy Pierce and his wife, Kristy. To them, life — and the taking of it — was not a debatable issue. The doctor informed them that their son would require numerous surgeries, would experience some cognitive problems, and might never walk. The first two statements proved true. But today, Jonathan is a happy six-year-old who loves to tickle his big brother and who not only walks, but runs. For the Pierces, the decision to choose life was not a difficult one.[8]

In Fran Caffey Sandin's book *Touching the Clouds*, Fran related another family's story, that of John and Jeanette Scott. Jeanette's obstetrician was not overly optimistic about her baby's future either, when chromosome tests confirmed their daughter, Anna, had Down's syndrome. She asked her doctor if Anna would go to school.

"No, I don't think so," he said thoughtfully, adding, "You'll be lucky if she does." But Anna exceeded the doctor's expectations.

"Anna's progress continued to the point she was able to attend a local private school from age three through five, and then she began public school. Her cheerful disposition and irrepressible smiles endeared her to me and to others as well.

"Her abilities continued to amaze us. I [Jeanette] taught piano lessons in our home after school, and apparently Anna had been listening carefully to the music. One day after a student had been playing 'Noel,' we were shocked when Anna later sat at the piano and began playing the same piece by ear. Then she played, 'Holy, Holy, Holy.' Her musical talent reminds us of our heavenly Father's creativity, and as she plays, she expresses love for Him."

Life is not something to discard, but a divine gift to regard with dignity, reverence, and wonder.

Now in her thirties, Anna lives in a group home and is "thriving there and becoming more independent every day." Jeanette would tell you that life through the years has been difficult and full of challenges. But she also says, "Since Anna was born into our family, I have learned so much that now I can truly thank God for the trials He has seen us through. He met our every need, whether it was financial or emotional.

"The Lord really got my attention one day through His Word:

'Did not he who made me in the womb make them? Did not the same one form us both within our mothers?'" (Job 31:15 NIV).[9]

Dr. Pierce says, "There is a cost to be paid for the decision you make." Every mom reading this book would agree. Life may be hard, but God is faithful. God needs all of us as women to encourage others with these truths. Life is not something to discard, but a divine gift to regard with dignity, reverence, and wonder.

Whatever your situation, he will make a way, and he will help you through the journey. I'm so glad that a young teenager named Mary believed that. And because of her decision to choose life, Jesus, the Son of God, was born.

The rest is history.

DAY-BREAK

Do you have a special-needs child or know others who have one? What challenges has God helped you through? How can you help those who are struggling with the decision of whether or not to choose life?

DAY-BRIEF

Every decision we make not only affects our future — but also that of others.

DAY-VOTEDLY YOURS

Jesus, I need your wisdom to make decisions in this life that will honor you. Help me to trust you for every challenge and difficulty in life. Thank you for your forgiveness and grace. Where would I be without you?

nothing but the truth

Trouble and distress have come upon me,
but your commands give me delight.
Psalm 119:143

I counted the articles in the morning newspaper. Almost without fail, every page contained a story of violence, injustice, or crime. New email warnings flood my computer weekly: "Women, beware!" Some new scam or crime has alerted users, and the warning circulates through cyberspace in record time.

By nature, women feel things deeply and recognize the injustices surrounding them. No one is exempt from these hard times. And the longer the world turns, the tougher the times are becoming. Crimes that once shocked and rocked commentators now appear as common events. And Christian women are among the victims. We have been — and all will be — affected. We will suffer loss; we will experience pain, illness, and death. Troubles will continue to stalk us like lions hunting their prey, because we live in a fallen world. That's the bad news.

But the good news is that in the midst of a sinful, confused world, we can find not despair, but delight — by clinging to God's truth. How is that possible?

In God's truth — his commands, his laws, his life, his provision

(Jesus) — we discover a joy in God's unchanging nature. His commands and his truths represent him, for he is the Word. God is both sovereign and good. If we look at the circumstances around us and invest our minds in fear and uncertainty, we will reap false and futile thinking. While we may always see a tension between the good and evil in this world, God's Word is filled with truth. And truth is the essence of who God is.

A. W. Tozer says, "That God is good is taught or implied on every page of the Bible and must be received as an article of faith as impregnable as the throne of God ... If God is not good, then there can be no distinction between kindness and cruelty, and heaven can be hell and hell, heaven. The goodness of God is the drive behind all the blessings He daily bestows upon us. God created us because He felt good in His heart and He redeemed us for the same reason."[10]

Truth is the essence of who God is.

Tozer adds, "Since God is immutable He never varies in the intensity of His loving-kindness. He has never been kinder than He now is, nor will He ever be less kind. He is no respecter of persons but makes His sun to shine on the evil as well as on the good, and sends His rain on the just and on the unjust. The cause of His goodness is in Himself; the recipients of His goodness are all His beneficiaries without merit and without recompense."[11]

So what does that mean to us? Our world may change, but God does not. Even in the worst of news, the truths in God's Word and knowing him bring the best into focus.

Life is never fair — but God *is* good. And that's a truth that brings great delight and peace, any way you look at it.

DAY-BREAK

How does the daily world news affect you? What truths in God's Word bring you the most delight?

DAY-BRIEF

Truth is not what you say; it's what God says — and who God is.

DAY-VOTEDLY YOURS

God, with you in control, I never need to be confused or anxious. Forgive me when I take my eyes off you and your Word, for it's in those pages of life that I find comfort, hope, and peace.

day 39
in the company of friends

A friend loves at all times.
Proverbs 17:17

You finally found a great friend. Then something happens. She or her husband gets transferred. Or one of them loses a job. Maybe there's a divorce. One of you moves away. She may even develop a serious illness. Death follows, and you lose someone close — again.

Most women have experienced the loss or change of at least one female relationship in their lives. "No big deal," they say. Who are we kidding? Women need other women. Friends *are* important.

In fact, Brenda Hunter says, as women, "our friends are important for our everyday survival ... Our friends are among our life's greatest treasures. They help us negotiate the difficult hurdles of life. What would we have done without friends in adolescence to help us navigate the travails of puberty and deal with our 'unreasonable' parents? And what about our twenty-something romances? Whom do we go to for emotional rescue when in the dating years the man of our dreams becomes the stuff of nightmares? We go to our friends. Later, they coach us through first-time motherhood. Years later as we help our kids pack for college, they witness our tears. Our friends walk with us through menopause as, once again, we are caught up in the hormonal crazies, and they listen as we fantasize about fleeing to the Caribbean or a convent.

"In their presence, we laugh about what drove us crazy hours before; with them we cry without shame, knowing we will be understood."[12]

We women need each other at all times, but especially in times of stress. When two biblical women suffered loss, how did their friendships affect their survival? After Naomi lost both her husband and sons, one daughter-in-law, Ruth, chose to go with Naomi back to her own land and people.

Naomi was returning home to her "girlfriends," but I wonder how many friends Ruth left behind. When they both arrived in Bethlehem, the women hardly recognized Naomi. But they listened to her cries of grief. What about Ruth? Surely life was different, and maybe lonely for her. She had Naomi's friendship, but she was still young and in need of other friends (Ruth 1).

But Naomi had a relative, Boaz, who owned a large grainfield. When she discovered Ruth had gleaned in his field one day (no doubt, a divine appointment), she, along with Boaz, encouraged Ruth to stick close to the other women workers there. There's safety in numbers — and in the company of other women friends (Ruth 2:1 – 9).

In times of difficulty, God supplied both women's needs. Not only did Ruth find new women friendships there in Bethlehem, she found a lifelong friend and husband in Boaz too (Ruth 4:13).

When "life" or death happens, and it will,
and friendships suffer a temporary or even permanent
loss, we can trust a God who knows our needs.

The last chapter of Ruth gives us a picture of Naomi's restored attitude as well as her renewed friendships. When Ruth bore Naomi a grandson, guess who celebrated with her? The same women who had listened to Naomi's bitter complaints offered this reminder and blessing: "Praise be to the LORD, who this day has not left you without a family guardian. May he become famous throughout Israel! He will renew your life and sustain you in your old age. For your daughter-in-law, who loves you and who is better to you than seven sons, has given him birth" (Ruth 4:14 – 15).

In our mobile society with emails, text messaging, and social networking websites, we can easily keep up with friends who move away. Some friends remain friends for life. Still, cyberspace and long-distance relationships are not the same as the girlfriend next door or across town.

When "life" or death happens, and it will, and friendships suffer a temporary or even permanent loss, we can trust a God who knows our needs. He may send you a totally unexpected relationship — like a Naomi mother-in-law or a Ruth daughter-in-law friendship. Or he may place you smack in the middle of a bunch of new women friends. And okay, if you're single, he might even provide a husband for you. But we're talking about *girl* friends here.

Either way, be encouraged. Ask — and watch for his provision. Jesus is your very best friend. And true friends never really leave or forsake you.

DAY-BREAK

In what ways do your women friendships help you survive

times of stress? What can you do this week to nurture your women friendships?

DAY-BRIEF

A girlfriend is someone who laughs with you, cries with you, and gives you chocolate.

DAY-VOTEDLY YOURS

Lord, thank you for the gift of women friendships. Help me to be the kind of friend to others that you are to me.

the last citation

The doorbell rang, but when I opened the door, the UPS man was driving away. I opened the priority envelope he left and was surprised to see a letter addressed to me from the president of Hardin-Simmons University, my alma mater. The words I read shocked me so much that I immediately dropped to my knees, sobbing. I was speechless.

If I were honest, when I was in high school and even in college, I probably thought that if there had been a page in the school annual showing the "Least Likely to Succeed," my picture might be on it. As a student my grades were great, but my confidence was not.

I went to college primarily to major in Larry, my high school sweetheart, who also attended HSU. But the classes I took and the teachers who taught me planted and cultivated seeds that would later grow and bloom in ways I never dreamed.

I earned my MRS. degree at the end of my freshman year, and I spent the next four and a half years working on my PhT (Putting Hubby Through), helping him finish college and seminary. It wasn't until I had been married a few years that I realized my high school love of English and reading translated into a passion for writing.

Children arrived, along with the challenges of motherhood. They grew up, and it was time to pay for *their* college costs. In addition to the busy demands of our church life, there never seemed to be time for me to go back to college full-time, and funding a degree hardly fit into our budget. I took a few classes and a writer's correspondence course along the way, but by the time I could afford college, my writing résumé already reflected what I loved doing, with some measure of success.

As a writer, I had won only two awards. One year as a young woman, I managed to win the "Persistence Award" at one of the many writers' conferences I attended — because I had netted over one thousand rejections in one year. I *was* a little compulsive back then. I sent greeting card ideas out in batches of fifteen or more, then circulated them often.

I determined to return to the same conference and win the most sales. I did, but they still called it the Persistence Award, because I also earned the most rejections — again. God taught me a valuable lesson that year, and one I've never forgotten. I discovered it was not how *much* I wrote but *why* I wrote (for his glory) and *whom* I wrote for (God alone) that made a difference. When I focused on making God's name known rather than my own, God changed me, and he changed my writing. (The next year they invited me back to the same writers' conference — this time to teach.)

In the years following that experience, I became a professional speaker and author of numerous books. "Persistence" had paid off.

Still, I found myself questioning God continually, "Are you sure this is what I need to be doing?" Maybe it was the lack of a "degree." I'm not sure. At any rate, I've always considered myself as simply an ordinary woman in love with an extraordinary God.

Perhaps that's why the letter I received from my university where I only attended one year seemed like such an unlikely announcement. I read the words again: "You've been selected to receive the HSU 2008 Distinguished Alumni Award in recognition of personal and professional accomplishments exemplary of the ideals and aims of the University."

Distinguished? Me? Not only could I not believe it; I even emailed the Alumni Association and asked if there had been some mistake.

"No," they assured me. "No mistake."

The weekend of the honor was such a surreal experience. At the banquet, the interim president read my citation, listing the reasons for my honor. Then in my short acceptance speech, I shared with the audience about my "Persistence Awards" and some of the detailed history I just told you.

> *Only one thing will matter then*
> *— what you did faithfully for his glory.*

When I sat down, the interim president, Dr. Jesse Fletcher, looked directly at me and grinned with a twinkle in his eye. "Rebecca," he said, "this is *not* a Persistence Award." That's when the tears flowed — again.

I do not tell you this story to boast. What could I ever boast about but the incredible faithfulness and goodness of God? No, I share it because some of you may be struggling wherever you are: in thankless jobs, in "no-honors" situations, in ordinary occupations, as a mom, a teacher, a single mother, or an aging senior, but you keep going, day after day because you love the Lord, and you are faithful to where he has placed you.

Your accolades might once have included "Senior Favorite," or maybe you graduated magna cum laude. You may have never finished high school, and some of you have papered the walls of your heart with rejection slips. But God has not forgotten you.

What I received was truly a gift — simply an honor I felt I did not deserve, but one that I could give back to God. And maybe for me, it was also God's final word to quiet my constant questioning after thirty years of writing: "Yes, my child. This (writing) *is* what I want you to be doing."

Earthly rewards will fade away. But someday, as beloved women and children of God, you will take your place among all the other honorees. Only one thing will really matter then — what you did faithfully for his glory. And every recipient who has known him and lived for him will be given a special honor, one that is exemplary of the ideals and aims of heaven.

As all of heaven witnesses, God will read your "citation" as Jesus says to you, "Well, done, good and faithful servant ... well done!"

DAY-BREAK

Draw a timeline of important events throughout your life.

Trace the faithful hand of God at work and spend a few moments celebrating and thanking him for the things — both small and great — he has done for you and through you.

DAY-BRIEF

The only applause that matters is God's "Well done!"

DAY-VOTEDLY YOURS

Lord, no matter where I've been or what I've done, you have walked beside me, guiding me, picking me up, and celebrating my successes. What would I do without you? Help me to always live a servant life worthy of your "Well done!"

epilogue

Perhaps you have never come to know and enjoy the intimate presence of God personally. If he has placed such a desire in your heart, may I share with you some simple steps so you can become acquainted with him and become a child of God forever?

1. Admit the sin in your life and the need in your heart for God (see Romans 3:23).
2. Acknowledge that Jesus loves you and that he died for your sin (see John 3:16).
3. Recognize his salvation is a gift, not something earned (see Romans 6:23; Ephesians 2:8 – 9).
4. Ask Jesus to forgive you, to come into your life, and to fill you with his personal, intimate presence (John 1:12).
5. By faith, thank him that you are now God's child, and confess that from now on, he will be the Lord and Love of your life. Give Jesus the keys to all the rooms of your heart (see Romans 10:9 – 10).

If this book has encouraged you, I'd love to hear from you. And if I can help you in your Christian growth in any way, please let me know. For more information, see my websites: www.rebeccabarlowjordan.com or www.day-votions.com

Rebecca Barlow Jordan

notes

1. "Trading Spouses," in Wikipedia, the free encyclopedia, en.wikipedia. org/wiki/Trading_Spouses (accessed February 16, 2009).

2. Bruce Wilkinson, *The Prayer of Jabez* (Sisters, Ore.: Multnomah, 2000), 29.

3. Ibid., 25–27.

4. E. C. McKenzie, *14,000 Quips and Quotes* (Peabody, Mass.: Hendrickson), 188.

5. "Reborn Doll," Wikipedia, the free encyclopedia, en.wikipedia.org/ wiki/Reborn_doll (accessed February 10, 2009).

6. Deborah Roberts, Gwen Gowen, and Rena Furuya, "Not Child's Play: 'I Feel Like I Have a Real Baby,'" on *20/20* (January 2, 2009) News:abcnews.go.com/2020/story?id+6517455&page=1 (2 & 3) (accessed February 10, 2009).

7. Michelle Blackshear, © 2008, http://3xlife.blogspot.com (accessed February 16, 2009). Used by permission.

8. Dr. Timothy Pierce, from his sermon at Highland Terrace Baptist Church, Greenville, Texas, on January 18, 2009. Used by permission.

9. Fran Caffey Sandin, *Touching the Clouds: Encouraging Stories to Make Your Faith Soar* (Colorado Springs: NavPress, 2003), 129, 132–34. Used with permission.

10. A. W. Tozer, *The Knowledge of the Holy* (New York: HarperSanFrancisco, 1961, 1992), 128.

11. Ibid., 130.

12. Brenda Hunter, *In the Company of Women* (Sisters, Ore.: Multnomah, 1994), 110.

endorsements

"I have watched, first-hand, the spiritual maturity and, now, the spiritual mastery of Rebecca Barlow Jordan. Hundreds of women of faith, in many parts of the world, will welcome her latest work.

I give a generous acknowledgment of God's hand on her as all her writings are rooted in experience. All of it is grounded in a remarkable grasp of the New Testament, giving it great impact in inspiring women with encouragement based on biblical truth."
—Jan Gott, international missions coordinator,
Michael Gott International

"Small adjustments often reap big rewards. So it is with *Day-votions™ for Women* by Rebecca Barlow Jordan. These simple, easy-to-read, daily inspirations are high-impact, high-octane fuel for the busy woman's day."
—Pam Farrel, bestselling author of *Men are like Waffles,
Women are like Spaghetti*; *Woman of Confidence*;
and *Devotions for Women on the Go*

Matt Christopher®

The #1 Sports Series for Kids

WORLD CUP

LITTLE, BROWN AND COMPANY
NEW YORK • BOSTON

Little, Brown and Company

Hachette Book Group
237 Park Avenue, New York, NY 10017
Visit our website at lb-kids.com

mattchristopher.com

Little, Brown and Company is a division of Hachette Book Group, Inc.
The Little, Brown name and logo are trademarks of Hachette Book Group, Inc.

The publisher is not responsible for websites (or their content) that are not owned
by the publisher.

First Edition: June 2010

Matt Christopher® is a registered trademark of Matt Christopher Royalties, Inc.

Library of Congress Cataloging-in-Publication Data

Christopher, Matt.
    World cup / Matt Christopher; [text written by] Stephanie True Peters.
        p. cm. — (Matt Christopher the #1 sports series for kids)
    ISBN 978-0-316-04484-4
    1. World Cup (Soccer) — History — Juvenile literature.   I. Peters, Stephanie
True.   II. Title.
    GV943.49.C47 2010
    796.334'66809 — dc22

                                                        2009035986

10 9 8 7 6 5 4 3

CW

Printed in the United States of America

Contents

WORLD CUP

⋆ INTRODUCTION ⋆

A Game for the Ages

In 1894, soccer was poised to join baseball, football, and basketball as one of the most popular sports in the United States. Everything pointed to its success. It had a set of standard rules, just like the others, and it had its own professional league, just like the others. The teams had access to newly constructed baseball stadiums, so finding big venues to play in wasn't a problem. And soccer had a widespread fan base, particularly among European immigrants setting up new lives in the United States. In their countries, soccer was king.

In the United States, however, soccer sank into virtual oblivion while baseball, football, and basketball rose to greatness. Why?

The answer seems to lie in the way the sport was handled. In Europe, soccer clubs were organized and managed by people who loved the game. Here, it was run by the baseball team owners who cared more about making money than they did about promoting soccer itself. When the first professional league failed to turn a profit, these men shut it down to focus on baseball.

While soccer was fading far into the background of the American sports scene, it was spreading like wildfire in many other countries. In fact, it was well on its way to becoming what it is today: the most popular sport on the planet.

The sport we call soccer and others call football was born on December 8, 1863, in Great Britain. On that day, a group of eleven English teams formed the London Football Association and published a set of rules by which the sport was to be played. Those rules were adopted by other countries in the coming decades, and while they have been modified since, they have remained essentially the same.

Soccer's roots stretch thousands of years further back in time, however. The oldest known form of the game, *t'su chu*, was played in ancient China as early as 2500 BC. Three thousand years later, the Japanese developed a different version of the game, called *kemari*, that was a combination of modern-day hacky sack and soccer. The ancient Greeks competed in their own kicking game called *episkyros*.

The Romans adopted the Greek sport, which they renamed *harpastum*. Harpastum was very popular with Roman soldiers. They introduced it to the peoples they conquered during the expansion of the Roman Empire, including those living on the British Isles. The Brits took to it right away—and soccer has been part of British culture, in one form or another, ever since.

The rules set down by the London Football Association in 1863 were quickly accepted by other countries. Soon, soccer blossomed from a club sport into an international phenomenon. To help fuel the fire, seven countries—France, Belgium, Denmark, Switzerland, the Netherlands, Spain, and Sweden—decided to create a governing organization for the sport. They founded the Fédération Internationale de Football Association, or FIFA, in Paris on May 21, 1904. Within the year, England, Scotland, Wales, Ireland, Austria, Hungary, Germany, and Italy had joined FIFA as well.

One of FIFA's first acts was to propose an annual championship tournament among the national teams. It wasn't a new idea. England and Scotland had played each other in just such a competition back in 1872. FIFA's tournament, however, would be on a much grander scale and therefore would, it was hoped, increase international interest in the sport even more.

The proposal was met with great enthusiasm. The inaugural competition was set for 1906.

But that competition never took place. It was canceled for one simple reason: none of the teams sent in applications! In the wake of such a colossal failure, the tournament idea was scrapped, to be revisited at a later date.

As it turned out, that date was much, much later. The 1908 and 1912 Olympics were in part to blame for the delay. After all, the Games included soccer matches between the best teams in the world, so why would another, very similar competition be necessary? Then, from 1914 to 1918, World War I threw many nations into utter chaos. After the war, the 1920 Olympics overshadowed all other international competitions.

In 1924, however, FIFA's new president, Jules Rimet, resurrected the tournament idea. Rimet wanted to turn soccer into an international sports sensation. The tournament was a big part of his plan to reach that goal.

The pieces fell into place soon after the 1924 Olympic soccer competition. The gold-medal winner was Uruguay, which played a fast-paced, thrilling style of soccer that captivated fans and left them clamoring for more. Rimet witnessed that enthusiasm and knew the time was right for FIFA's tournament.

A Uruguayan diplomat named Enrique Buero agreed. He, too, had seen the crowds cheering for his country's players. At the time, Uruguay was struggling to be accepted into international circles, but soccer had pushed his nation into the limelight as nothing else ever had. Buero realized that if Uruguay hosted FIFA's tournament, the country would gain the attention it needed.

Buero approached Rimet with an offer to hold FIFA's tournament in Uruguay in 1930, his country's one hundredth birthday. Rimet was delighted but cautious. After all, while he wanted the tournament to happen, FIFA hadn't seriously considered the idea for nearly twenty years. And even if the Fédération did decide to hold the competition, there was no guarantee that it would accept Uruguay as the host nation.

The first hurdle was jumped in 1927, when FIFA officially agreed to pursue a world championship. The second hurdle, however, proved more difficult.

In 1929, five other countries expressed interest in playing host. It took all of Rimet's powers of persuasion to convince them to withdraw. When they did, Uruguay was selected as the host of the first FIFA tournament—or "World Cup" as it was already being called.

But selecting a country in which to play soccer and actually *playing* in that country turned out to be two very different things. In 1929, Europe and the

United States were wading waist-deep in economic disaster, and most of their players could not afford a journey to South America. The trip to Uruguay was also very time consuming; it would leave many European teams without their best players for two months.

As the date for the World Cup neared, the European teams began pushing for a change of location.

"Hold the World Cup in Rome," they suggested, "and then we'll play."

But by then, plans were already in place for Uruguay to host. Changing the location, with the tournament so near, was not feasible.

Once more Rimet stepped in. He managed to get four European nations — Belgium, France, Romania, and Yugoslavia — to commit to playing in the tournament in Uruguay. With the United States, Mexico, and seven South American countries also on board, that brought the total number of teams competing in the first-ever World Cup to thirteen.

It had taken twenty-four years — or thousands, if you went back in time far enough — but at last, the dream of an international soccer competition was about to come true.

★ CHAPTER ONE ★

1930

The Host Is the Most

On July 15, 1930, Argentina and France met to play the second game of the first World Cup—a match that would go down in soccer history, not because of its exciting action or high score, but because it produced one of the oddest endings to any match ever played.

The teams were equals in every way, leading to a scoreless first half. It wasn't until the eighty-one-minute mark, in fact, that Argentina's Luisito Monti booted the ball into the net. Argentina 1, France 0.

France redoubled its efforts and, as the clock wound down to the final minutes, got within striking range of Argentina's goal. They had just launched their attack when suddenly the referee blew his whistle to signal that the game was over. Time, it seemed, had run out for the French.

Or had it? It turned out that the referee had misread the clock. There were actually six minutes left to play!

Players were called back to the field—some of them out of the locker-room showers—and the game resumed half an hour later. Much to France's disappointment, however, the final result was the same. Argentina defeated them, 1–0.

France's loss came on the second day of the 1930 World Cup. That same week, nine of the thirteen participating teams were forced out of the competition, leaving Yugoslavia, Uruguay, and the United States to join Argentina in the semifinal round.

That two South American teams, Uruguay and Argentina, had made it so far in the competition was no surprise. After all, Uruguay was the reigning Olympic champion and boasted top scorer Pedro Cea. Argentina had offensive might, too, including Luisito Monti and Guillermo Stábile, who was nicknamed *El Infiltrador,* or "the Infiltrator," for his ability to worm his way past the defense.

The United States, still a newcomer to soccer, had reached the semifinals by literally muscling its way past the competition. Its players were big, but not as skilled as those on other teams. Argentina ran roughshod over them, outscoring the bewildered Americans six goals to one.

Yugoslavia was a surprise team and something of a mystery to the other nations. No one had seen enough of its style of play to know how it might fare against Uruguay. But how it fared was badly: the host country trounced the Yugoslavs, 6–1.

That victory set the stage for one of the most anticipated and highly charged finals the soccer world had ever known.

Uruguay and Argentina had been rivals on and off the pitch for years. All of South America was watching to see which country would come out on top. Nothing less than national pride was on the line.

In fact, when the Uruguayans found out that Argentina's star player, veteran Pancho Varallo, had a broken foot, they rejoiced in the streets. In response, the Argentine coach ordered Varallo to play despite his injury. To do otherwise, the coach intimated, would make Argentina appear weak.

Eighty thousand fans packed into Centenario Stadium, a brand-new arena built especially for the finals (and completed just days before the match!). Emotions in the stands were running hot—so hot, in fact, that police were ordered to search spectators for weapons in order to prevent violence.

The first World Cup finals began at three thirty on July 30. Within the first minutes, Argentina lost one of its key players when Varallo fell to the ground, writhing in pain from his foot injury.

The loss of Varallo gave Uruguay an instant boost. Twelve minutes into the first half, they attacked the goal. Pablo Dorado got his foot on the ball and kicked. One second later, Uruguay was on the board—and Dorado was in the record books for scoring the first-ever World Cup finals goal.

But Argentina didn't let up. Eight minutes later, Carlos Peucelle answered with a goal for his side. *El Infiltrador* added a second one for Argentina and caused the first disagreement of the game in doing so. Uruguay claimed that Argentina had been offside—that is, there hadn't been two defenders between the offensive player and the goalie when the shooter received the pass. Therefore, they argued, the goal didn't count.

But the referee stood by his call. The goal stayed on the board.

Argentina went into the second half with a one-point lead over the world champion. They didn't keep that lead for long, however. At the fifty-seven-minute mark, Pedro Cea of Uruguay booted the ball into the net to tie the game. Eleven minutes after that, team-mate Santos Iriarte did the same. Now Uruguay had the lead, 3–2!

That was too much for Pancho Varallo to bear. He signaled to his coach that he wanted to go back into the game, pain or no. When he limped onto the field, he did more than change the lineup: he brought new life back to the flagging Argentines, inspiring them to play harder. He himself played as hard as he could despite his injury and, late in the game, very nearly tied the score.

In fact, according to Vallaro, he *had* tied the score. Uruguay's goalkeeper, he argued, had knocked one of his shots back *after* it had crossed the goal line. But once again, the referee had the final word on the play. He said the ball had been deflected *before* it crossed the line and, therefore, was not a goal.

Uruguay sealed the win with another goal a minute before the game ended, making the final score Uruguay 4, Argentina 2. The Olympic champs were victorious again!

Raucous celebrations erupted throughout the stadium, in the streets, and throughout the host country. Jules Rimet presented the Victory Cup (renamed the Jules Rimet Cup in 1946) to the Uruguayan Football Association's president, beginning a tradition that remains unbroken today.

By all accounts, the first World Cup had been a huge triumph for the sport of soccer. The only question now was, how could FIFA build on this success and make the second competition even better?

✴ CHAPTER TWO ✴

1934

Welcome to Italy

The first World Cup had seen participation by only thirteen teams. Four years later, despite troubles caused by the crumbling world economy, a total of thirty-two nations sent in applications to take part in the 1934 World Cup.

FIFA was delighted that interest in soccer had grown so dramatically. But a pool of thirty-two teams was simply too large for one event (or so they thought at the time; later on, thirty-two teams would seem just right). So the Fédération decided to hold a series of qualifying rounds to whittle the number of participants to sixteen. That practice continues on a much larger scale today.

Sadly, one team chose not to take part in the competition at all. Uruguay had felt insulted when some European countries, including Italy, had refused to travel to South America for the 1930 World Cup. When Italy was chosen as the host for 1934, Uruguay withdrew in retaliation.

Uruguay wasn't the only nation dismayed by the choice of Italy. FIFA itself had some serious misgivings about the host. It wasn't the country's ability to hold the tournament that concerned the Fédération, but its leader, Benito Mussolini. Mussolini was a fierce dictator intent on turning Italy into a dominant world power (Mussolini would later side with Adolf Hitler and Nazi Germany during World War II). FIFA feared Mussolini would use the World Cup to promote his goals. But unfortunately, no other nation stepped forward to play host; it was Italy or nowhere.

Italy welcomed fifteen other national teams to the second World Cup. Twelve of those teams, including the host nation, were from Europe. The remaining four were the United States, Argentina, Brazil, and the first African nation to compete, Egypt.

Play began on May 27 with eight elimination matches taking place in eight different Italian cities. At the end of the day, Italy, Germany, Czechoslovakia, Austria, Spain, Sweden, Switzerland, and Hungary emerged victorious. These eight teams competed in a second elimination round that left Italy, Czechoslovakia, Austria, and Germany standing while the others returned home.

Next up was the semifinal round. The first match saw Czechoslovakia beating Germany three goals to one. Then came the most anticipated match of the competition between the sport's two biggest power-houses, Austria and Italy.

Austria used an innovative offense based on short passes, a strategy perfected by its best player, Matthias Sindelar. With Sindelar leading the charge, the Austrian team had won eighteen consecutive games. One of those victories was a 4–2 win over Italy four months earlier. The Austrians entered the match hoping to hand the Italians another defeat.

Italy looked more than able to deny them that satisfaction, however. Thanks to a unique law that allowed people to claim Italian citizenship if they could prove they descended from an Italian family, their roster was stacked with talented imports that included star Luisito Monti as well as fellow Argentine Raimondo Orsi. Leading the charge was coach Vittorio Pozzo, who had single-handedly launched his country's soccer program years earlier.

The Italian team got a break even before the match began. One of Austria's top scorers, Johann Horvath, was sidelined with an injury. As an added bonus, the pitch was a soggy, muddy mess. The field conditions slowed Austria's short-passing game and made Monti's job of disarming Sindelar's attack that much easier.

Italy scored first. The goal came when the ball

squeaked past Austria's goalkeeper to reach Italy's Enrico Guaita. All Guaita had to do was knock the ball into the net—which he did.

Try as they might, the Austrians couldn't even things up. After ninety minutes of rough play, Italy was on the way to the finals to face Czechoslovakia.

The game was played on June 10 in Rome in front of a stadium packed with fifty thousand fans, including Benito Mussolini and Jules Rimet. All probably assumed they would see an offensive duel—certainly a possibility considering Czechoslovakian player Oldřich Nejedlý was the Cup's top scorer so far with five goals, while Angelo Schiavio had three and Orsi two for Italy.

Instead, what they saw was a defensive standoff. After more than seventy minutes, neither team had scored! Then finally, with fourteen minutes remaining, Antonin Puc of Czechoslovakia slipped a low drive past Italian goalkeeper and team captain Giampiero Combi. The Czechs were on the scoreboard and were very close to adding a second goal when one of their shots rebounded off the post.

In the stands, Mussolini sat in stony silence. He was not a soccer fan, but with national pride on the line, he wanted his team to win. According to some, he had made it clear to coach Pozzo that defeat would not be tolerated.

Luckily for Pozzo, Orsi wanted to win just as badly. At the eighty-one-minute mark, he took a shot. And what a shot it was! Rather than sailing on a line, it spiraled weirdly, baffling the Czech goalkeeper, who hesitated for a split second before acting. By then, he was too late: the ball was in the net and the score was tied!

It remained tied through the remaining minutes, forcing a thirty-minute overtime, scheduled to take place the next day. It took just five minutes of that time for Italy's Schiavio to deliver the winning goal. Czechoslovakia couldn't answer. Italy was the World Cup champion!

While the host country celebrated its victory, Rimet began to plan for the third FIFA championship, scheduled to be held in 1938. But even the best-laid plans can go awry. In the years that followed, events began to unfold that would have an impact on soccer — and the world.

∗ CHAPTER THREE ∗

1938

"Win or Die"

When FIFA published the schedule for the 1938 World Cup preliminary matches, Austria was listed among the participating nations. On October 5, 1937, the team beat Latvia to earn one of the sixteen finalist slots.

But when the World Cup began in early June of 1938, Austria was not among the competitors—because Austria no longer existed as a nation. It had been forcibly reunified with Germany three months earlier. The reunification, called the *Anschluss,* had been orchestrated by Germany's dictator, Adolf Hitler, as the first major step toward his goal of world domination.

The reunification extended to Austria's and Germany's soccer programs. After the Anschluss, Austria's best players were cherry-picked to strengthen Germany's roster.

One of those players, Matthias Sindelar, refused to accept Hitler's "invitation" to play for Germany, however. He claimed that his decision was based on his age, not his politics. Still, Sindelar made it clear that he opposed Hitler and his agenda. He even went out of his way to greet the former chairman of the Austrian team, who was Jewish, despite being ordered to ignore the man.

"The new chairman has forbidden me to greet you," he said, "but I, Herr Doktor, will always greet you."

Less than a year later, Sindelar was discovered in his apartment dead from carbon-monoxide poisoning. His death was ruled an accident, but rumors have persisted to this day that he was killed for his defiance or that perhaps he committed suicide.

Even without Sindelar, the German squad promised to be a powerhouse in the competition. And that was exactly what Hitler wanted it to be. After all, domination in the world of soccer was a small but significant part of his plan to dominate the world itself.

But Italy's ruler, Benito Mussolini, wasn't about to let Hitler's German team steal the Cup from Italy without a fight. He sent the defending champions to the competition with a three-word message: "Win or Die." According to some historians, this message simply meant "do your best to be victorious." Given the political tensions of the time, however, some of the players may have taken the words much more literally!

The third World Cup was held in France. The first round of play began on June 4 with a match between Switzerland and Germany. The game ended in a 1–1 tie, forcing a rematch four days later. That day, the Swiss team bested the German squad decisively, 4–2 — despite becoming the first squad in the history of the World Cup to score an "own goal" when they kicked the ball into their own net! With the loss, Hitler's quest to rule the world of soccer ended in failure.

In the meantime, on June 5, France beat Belgium, Hungary annihilated the Dutch East Indies, Italy defeated Norway, the Netherlands fell to Czechoslovakia, and Cuba tied Romania, forcing another rematch. But by far the most exciting game of the first round was between Brazil and Poland.

Brazil was South America's only representative that year. Argentina had qualified, but when Jules Rimet chose France as the host country, the Argentines withdrew in anger. They had been led to believe that the Cup's location would alternate between Europe and the Americas, and they had petitioned hard to play host. Understandably, they were infuriated that a European nation had been selected for the second time in a row. Other countries from Central and

North America, including the United States, sided with Argentina and withdrew after qualifying.

But Brazil's opponent, Poland, was eager to play in its first World Cup. After suffering elimination in the qualifying rounds in 1934, it had fought hard to reach the final competition this year.

The match, held in Strasbourg in driving rain, was an offensive battle from the start. Brazil struck first with a goal off the foot of Leônidas Da Silva. Leônidas was nicknamed the "Rubber Man" because of the way he bent around defenses. Among his other legendary achievements, Leônidas perfected the bicycle kick later made famous by another Brazilian — Pelé.

Leônidas's goal came eighteen minutes into the game. But Poland's Fryedryk Szerfke answered five minutes later with a penalty goal to tie the score.

Brazil fought back, chalking up two more goals to end the first half with a satisfying 3–1 lead. That gap shrank eight minutes into the second half, when Ernest Wilimowski of Poland walloped one into the net. The lead disappeared completely when Wilimowski booted in another goal six minutes later.

Brazil got the upper hand again at the seventy-one-minute mark with a goal by José Perácio, his second of the game. As the clock ticked steadily through the remaining time, they held on to the one-point lead. With one minute left to play, a victory for the South Americans seemed assured.

But then—*whomp!* Wilimowski scored yet *another* goal. Tie score!

With two other tiebreaker matches already scheduled, FIFA decided to continue the game that day. Leônidas came out kicking, delivering two goals in quick succession to put Brazil ahead and earn him a hat trick (three goals in one game).

Poland couldn't recover, although Wilimowski did what no player had yet to do in a World Cup, namely, score four goals in one game. His fourth and final goal came with less than two minutes remaining. It was a fantastic achievement, but just not enough. Final score: Brazil 6, Poland 5.

After such excitement early on in the competition, the games that followed were something of a letdown—particularly for Czechoslovakia, who lost to Brazil in a second round tie-breaker, and Cuba, who lost to Sweden, 8–0. One by one, other teams fell too until only Italy and Hungary remained.

From the start, the Italians were the heavy favorites. Not only had they taken the World Cup in 1934, they were also the gold-medal winners of the 1936 Olympics. Their players, coached by veteran Vittorio

Pozzo, had several years of experience under their belts. They knew one another's style of play and they knew how to pick apart their opposition.

In the final match, they put that experience and knowledge to work right away with a goal by Gino Colausi on an assist by Giuseppe Meazza. Meazza was a stellar player, a "born forward" according to Pozzo, and the team's captain. He was also cool as a cucumber in stressful situations, as evidenced by one of the more memorable moments of the 1938 World Cup.

Midway through the semifinal game against Brazil, Meazza was tapped to take a penalty shot. But before he could put the ball in position, his shorts fell down! Apparently, the elastic waistband had been torn earlier in the game; now, in front of thousands of spectators, it had finally given way.

Meazza didn't seem fazed by the embarrassing situation, however. He simply hiked up his drawers, set the ball on the ground, and then calmly booted a shot past the astonished goalkeeper.

Fortunately for Italian fans, Meazza's uniform stayed put throughout the finals. He assisted on two more goals, one by Silvio Piola, the other by Colausi again, to give his team a 3–1 lead before the half.

The win wasn't in Italy's pocket yet. After the half, Hungary drew within one on a goal by György Sárosi.

But as the final ten minutes ticked down, Piola made his second goal of the game to give Italy 4 on their side of the scoreboard.

Try as they might, the Hungarian players just couldn't make up the difference. When the whistle blew to end the game, the Italians had successfully defended their title as champions of the world!

The Hungarians were, no doubt, disappointed to have come in second. But at least one player tried to see the bigger picture. Referring to Mussolini's "win or die" message, goalkeeper Antal Szabo reportedly quipped, "We may have lost the match, but we saved eleven lives."

What Szabo didn't know—what no one knew—was that all too soon, many, many more than eleven lives would be lost. Within a year, the political tensions that had been simmering throughout Europe began to boil; by 1941, they had erupted into the most catastrophic conflict the world had ever known: World War II.

The Second World War raged throughout Europe, Asia, and Africa for the next four years. Millions of lives were lost and countless cities and towns destroyed. After the war finally ended, it took these nations many long years to recover.

The sporting world suffered losses, too. Athletes from all corners of the globe had joined the fight;

thousands never returned from the battlefronts. Those who did survive returned crippled, physically and mentally, or too far past their prime to ever participate in their sport again. Highly anticipated international events, such as the 1940 and 1944 Olympic Games, were canceled. So, too, were the 1942 and 1946 World Cup tournaments.

In fact, it would be twelve years before the World Cup was played again.

⋆ CHAPTER FOUR ⋆

1950

The Miracle and the Defeat

The Second World War officially ended on September 2, 1945. Less than a year later, FIFA held its twenty-fifth Congress in Luxembourg. Several decisions were made at the meeting, including changing the name of the World Cup trophy to the Jules Rimet Cup, selecting Brazil as the host of the next tournament, and declaring Spanish the official language of the organization. But the most newsworthy accomplishment was the readmittance of the four nations of the British Isles.

At the time, England, Scotland, Ireland, and Wales had some of the biggest and best soccer programs in the world. But they had not been part of FIFA for nearly twenty years because of disagreements concerning the use of amateur players. In 1946, those disagreements were finally resolved, thanks in large part to negotiations by Rimet. To seal the deal, the English team faced off against a team made up of eleven FIFA players in 1947. England won the so-called "Match of the Century" 6–1, proof positive that it was one of the top-notch teams around.

But England wasn't the only powerhouse. Thirty-four nations submitted entries for the preliminary rounds of the next World Cup competition, set for 1950. Of the fourteen teams that qualified for the sixteen slots — the other two slots were automatically filled by Brazil, the host country, and Italy, the defending champion — only eleven wound up participating in the Cup. India, Scotland, and Turkey had chosen to withdraw, and although invitations were extended to France and Portugal, neither accepted.

With an uneven field of thirteen teams, the 1950 World Cup followed an unusual format. The teams were divided into four pools, two with four teams each, one with three, and one with just two. The surviving team from each pool would then play in a round-robin final.

Because of its long soccer history and the obvious skill of its players, England was judged as a top contender. But host nation Brazil was high on the list as well and was by far the favorite among soccer-crazy South Americans. Even before competition began, many were predicting that one of these two countries would reign victorious.

Those predictions would not come true, however. In fact, England wouldn't even make it into the final round! The defeat of the English team was even more shocking because it was handed to them, in part, by a very unlikely source: the United States.

Soccer was still very low on the totem pole of U.S. sports in 1950. The U.S. national team was talented but mostly unsupported by the public. Few people even knew there was such a team, let alone cared about its chances to win a competition taking place in a distant country.

But the players themselves cared. Despite clearly being the underdogs of the tournament, they set out to play their hardest. If they were defeated, as everyone assumed they would be, they would at least know they had given it everything they had.

True to expectations, the U.S. team lost its first match to Spain, 3–1. Four days later, the Americans faced England—and delivered one of the greatest upsets the World Cup had, or has, ever known.

On one side of the pitch were the English players, dedicated and highly paid professional athletes who were insured against injury to the tune of three million dollars. On the other were the Americans, a motley crew of amateurs who worked regular jobs for their daily pay.

One of those players was Joseph Gaetjens. Gaetjens was born in Haiti but moved to New York to attend Columbia University. He got a job as a dishwasher in a Brooklyn restaurant to pay his bills. In his free time, he played for one of the city's soccer teams, Brookhattan, where he came to the attention of the U.S. national team's coach in 1949. (Although Gaetjens wasn't a U.S. citizen, he was allowed to join the team just by expressing interest in becoming one.)

The match between England and the United States took place on June 29 before a crowd of ten thousand spectators. The English began their attack right away, dodging around the U.S. defense and firing off shot after shot on Frank Borghi, the U.S. goalkeeper. But to their surprise and dismay, Borghi fended off their attempts. The one shot that looked to be an easy goal instead clanged off the post.

That missed opportunity gave the Americans a much-needed confidence boost. After several minutes of lackluster play, they suddenly came to life. Then, at the thirty-seven-minute mark, midfielder Walter Bahr kicked the ball from twenty-five yards out.

What happened next has gone down in soccer history.

Bert Williams, the English goalkeeper, moved to make the save. At the same time, Gaetjens flew across the field. He dove at the ball and met it with his head. That hit sent the ball on a completely different trajectory—namely, away from Williams and into the net!

The English players were stunned. The *United States* had scored against *them?* Impossible! And what was even more impossible was the fact that England didn't answer that goal with any of its own! Final score: United States 1, England 0.

That's the headline British citizens were greeted with the next morning. Most figured the score had been a typo; the *real* score had to have been England *10,* United States 1. Imagine their shock when they learned the truth!

But their shock was nothing compared to that of many Brazilians two weeks later.

The host country had mounted a strong campaign in the first round to advance to the finals. On the way, they annihilated Sweden, 7–1, and then dispatched Spain, 6–1. Because of the way the World Cup was scored—a win earned a team two points, a draw one, and a loss zero—Brazil entered its final match, against Uruguay, needing only a draw to take the championship.

The game between Brazil and Uruguay was scheduled for three o'clock on July 16. The stadium, Maracana, was crammed to capacity with more than two hundred thousand screaming fans, many of whom had arrived hours earlier, certain they would soon be celebrating their nation's victory over Uruguay. One newspaper echoed that confidence and preprinted its morning edition announcing Brazil as the new World Cup champion.

Needing just a draw, Brazil could easily have played a purely defensive game. But that wasn't how the players wanted to win, so instead they peppered the Uruguayan goalkeeper with multiple shots in the first half. To their surprise, and the crowd's growing dismay, none of those shots found the back of the net.

It wasn't until two minutes into the second half that the spectators got what they wanted.

"Zizinho passed to me," forward Albino Friaça Cardosa recalled years later, referring to his teammate Thomaz Soares da Silva, aka Zizinho, "and I went past their right winger and their center half. I came into their box, and I shot."

Goal!

The fans erupted with joyful cheers. Confetti and ribbons rained down on the field. Gunpowder explosions sent clouds of smoke billowing over the stands.

But, as one Brazilian later observed, "We forgot something very important. This Uruguayan team was excellent. And our team wasn't as excellent as we thought."

One Uruguayan player suddenly started to cause trouble for the Brazilians. Right winger Alcides Ghiggia was an excellent dribbler and playmaker. At the sixty-six-minute mark, he put both skills to use.

He dribbled the ball around a defender who slipped trying to stop him. Then he crossed the touchline and sent the ball to his teammate Juan Schiaffino. Schiaffino turned, aimed, and shot. The ball soared past Brazil's keeper, Moacir Barbosa Nascimento, and swished against the net strings.

The Brazilians had hoped to go out with a win, but a draw was fine too since it would still give them the championship. All they had to do was prevent Uruguay from scoring another goal in the next twenty-four minutes.

They didn't. With eleven minutes remaining, Ghiggia struck again.

A short, grainy, black-and-white film clip, eerily silent, captured the historic moment. Ghiggia collected the ball on the right wing, saw the defense out of position, and kicked. The ball rose a foot off the ground and curled toward the net. Barbosa, alone in front of the net, couldn't make the save. Goal for Uruguay!

The fans, so raucous just seconds before, fell into a deep, shocked silence—a silence that continued through the rest of the game and for many days afterward throughout the streets of Rio de Janeiro and in the country beyond. After all, no one in Brazil had reason to cheer. Their team, their pride and glory, had been defeated, two goals to one.

☆ CHAPTER FIVE ☆

1954

The Mighty Fall

When FIFA met in 1946 they selected Brazil as the host country for the 1950 World Cup and Switzerland for the 1954 contest. The number of entrants for the second postwar competition grew from thirty-four in 1950 to forty-five in 1954. Unlike the 1950 Cup, which saw only thirteen teams in the tournament, this Cup had all sixteen slots filled, making it easier for FIFA to format the rounds of play. The sixteen teams were split into four groups of four for the first round. Two winners from each group moved on to the quarterfinals; the four teams that then emerged victorious went on to semifinal play, with the top two advancing to the finals.

This year's tournament saw three newcomers to the field, the most notable being Scotland. Scotland, like its neighbor England, had a long and fruitful soccer past. Many expected the nation to do well.

It did not. In its first match it faced Austria (which had been declared an independent country again after World War II, even as Germany was being divided into East and West) and lost, 1–0. Then it was stunned by the defending champion, Uruguay, by a demoralizing seven goals to none.

It may have been small consolation to the Scots when other teams lost by equal or even greater margins. In Group 2, the Korea Republic—making its first World Cup appearance—fell twice, once to Hungary, 9–0, and then to Turkey, 7–0. The Turks discovered how humiliating such a loss could be when, three days later, they were crushed by the West Germans, 7–2. West Germany could have sympathized, however, having lost to Hungary, 8–3, in earlier play!

Scores like these, more typical of baseball games than soccer matches, had fans jumping with excitement and defenders scratching their heads in bewilderment. But the shoot-out wasn't over yet. In the first game of the quarterfinals, Switzerland landed an amazing three goals in the first nineteen minutes of play. Normally, those goals would have given the Swiss an insurmountable lead. But the host country's defense fell apart in the ten minutes before halftime, giving up five goals to Austria! The Austrians took the game, 7–5—a tournament record number of goals in one game.

The other quarterfinal matches weren't quite as

high scoring. When the dust had settled, Austria was joined by West Germany, Hungary, and Uruguay in the semifinals. Left behind with Switzerland were England, Brazil, and Yugoslavia. This last team had surprised many by beating out France and tying Brazil earlier in the tournament.

Of the final four teams, the Hungarians were considered to be the best. They were the gold-medal champs of the 1952 Summer Olympics, had a four-year record of twenty-three wins and four draws, and had recently beaten England at Wembley Stadium — the first time any visiting team had ever defeated the English on their home soil. It came as no surprise to anyone, therefore, that Hungary advanced to the semifinals by beating Brazil and then to the finals, where it faced West Germany.

The Germans ran onto the pitch burning to reverse their humiliating 8–3 loss to Hungary. But at least one Hungarian player was equally eager for revenge. Team captain Ferenc Puskás had been hacked by Germany's center half in their earlier meeting. He'd sat out the quarterfinal and semifinal games, nursing an injured ankle. When the Hungarians won their way to the finals without him, he was delighted — and determined to join the team on the field regardless of the pain.

The Germans were delighted to have him in the

opposing lineup. A formidable foe when healthy, the limping Puskás would no doubt do more harm than good for the Hungarians.

But as it turned out, all the players would have trouble with their footing in that final game. Rain had started before the game and continued throughout, turning the pitch into a slippery, muddy mess that found more than one player landing face-first in the slop.

If Puskás was bothered by the mud or his ankle injury, he didn't show it. Instead, he attacked the Germans' goal and, in the sixth minute, scored! Less than two minutes later, the Hungarians added a second goal when Germany's keeper bobbled the ball right in front of Zoltán Czibor. All the forward from Hungary had to do was knock it into the net, which he did.

The Germans didn't give up, however. They chalked up two of their own to tie the game, 2–2, at the break.

Defense took center stage in the second half of the game, with neither team able to break the tie. Then, as the clock clicked into the eighty-fourth minute of the match, Germany's right forward, Helmut Rahn, raced in, claimed the ball with his left foot, and kicked.

Thump! The shot sailed into the far corner of the goal! The West Germans had the lead!

Puskás made one final, desperate attempt to level the score. He might have succeeded, too, but for one small problem: the referee whistled him offside when he made his shot. Although the ball swished into the net, it was discounted. Minutes later, the game ended. The Germans had beaten the seemingly unbeatable Hungarians, 3–2.

As was traditional, aging FIFA president Jules Rimet presented the Cup to the winning coach. It was a bittersweet moment for Rimet. After thirty-three years as FIFA's leader, he was retiring from the organization. Handing over the Cup was his last official act.

Rimet died just two years later. Thanks to his efforts, soccer and the World Cup had gained world-wide recognition. Sadly, however, he passed away without ever meeting the player who would single-handedly catapult international soccer into the sports stratosphere.

★ CHAPTER SIX ★

1958

What's in a Name?

Edson Arantes do Nascimento doesn't know how he got his nickname. He doesn't know what it means, either. But he does know he didn't like it at first. He got used to hearing it over time, however—lucky considering it was the name hundreds of thousands of people screamed for decades during soccer games. In fact, ask most people to name one soccer player, and it's the name they'll give you:

"PELÉ!"

Pelé was born on October 23, 1940, in a small town in Brazil. He grew up poor, with no money for soccer equipment. That didn't stop him from playing his favorite game, though. He and his friends made balls out of old socks stuffed with newspapers. They formed teams and played barefoot on dusty dirt roads. His happiest days were the ones when he played soccer from sunup to sundown.

Even as a youngster, Pelé was remarkably talented. He was just fifteen years old when a famous soccer player named Valdemar de Brito discovered him. De Brito helped Pelé get on a professional team called Santos, named after the team's hometown.

Pelé played for Santos from 1956 until 1974. He also played on Brazil's national team during those years. It was as a member of that squad that he first caught the attention of the world.

Pelé was seventeen years old when he traveled to Sweden for the 1958 World Cup. As in 1954, all sixteen slots were filled, allowing for the same format of four pools of four teams for the initial rounds of play. Brazil was grouped with Austria, England, and the Soviet Union.

The Soviets were making their first appearance in the Cup. They beat out England to advance to the quarterfinals. England's loss didn't come as a surprise, but it did sadden many soccer fans. On February 6, 1958, the English team had suffered a tragedy when a plane carrying forty-four people crashed. Twenty-three passengers perished, eight of whom were English soccer players. The team simply couldn't recover, emotionally or practically, after such a tremendous loss.

The Soviet Union didn't move beyond the quarterfinals, however, being beaten by Sweden. Brazil stayed alive with a 1–0 victory over Wales, which was also in the World Cup for the first time. France and defending champion West Germany also reached the semifinal round.

On June 24, the Germans battled the Swedes in an exciting match that was tied at the half. But Germany couldn't survive the host nation's onslaught. They allowed two goals in the remaining forty-five minutes while failing to put one in their opponents' net. Sweden was through to the finals.

Meanwhile, on that same day in the city of Solna, twenty-seven thousand fans witnessed the emergence of soccer's superstar.

Brazil had drawn France as its opponent in the semifinal round. With two high-scoring games under their belts in the tournament, the French players hit the field full of confidence. Brazil quickly deflated them, however, with a goal a mere two minutes into play. But France answered soon after to tie things up. Then Brazil's star player, Didi (born Valdir Pereira), blasted one into the net at the thirty-nine-minute mark.

A one-goal lead is nice, but not impossible to overcome. No one knew that better than Brazil's youngest player. Pelé had watched his team from the sidelines in earlier games, nursing a knee injury. Fortunately, he was back on the field in time to play against the Soviets in the third game. He had played well that match, working in tandem with another of the team's stars, Manuel "Garrincha" dos Santos, but he hadn't been a standout. People started to sit up and take notice of him in the quarterfinal against Wales, however, when he scored the game's single goal.

But it was in the second half of the semifinal against France that he truly stormed the scene. Within twenty-three minutes he scored not one, not two, but *three* goals! He was the youngest player in World Cup history to earn a hat trick. France simply couldn't stop him. The final score was Brazil 5, France 2.

Sweden and Brazil met on June 29. More than fifty thousand fans crowded into the stadium in Solna. Countless others watched from the comfort of their homes, for the World Cup was being televised internationally for the first time ever. Black-and-white film footage of the game, which still exists, captured each goal as well as the reactions of the players and the spectators.

The Swedes drew first blood with a slashing shot by Nils Liedholm just four minutes into the game. The score didn't stay at 1–0 for long. Less than five minutes later Garrincha snared the ball, flew down the right sideline, cut toward the goal, and threaded a pass through the defense to his teammate Edvaldo Izídio Neto, or Vavá as he was known. Vavá sent the ball right into the net to tie the game at one apiece.

It was Garrincha to Vavá again twenty-three minutes later with an almost identical play resulting in Brazil's second goal. The first half ended with the score still at Brazil 2, Sweden 1.

That's where it stayed through the first ten minutes of the second half. Then, with the clock showing fifty-five, Pelé received a high pass in front of the goal. As defenders swarmed to cover him, he bounced the ball once on his thigh and then sent it arcing over the closest Swede. As the Swedish player's momentum carried him forward, Pelé dodged around, retrieved the ball, and powered it with a mighty kick into the goal.

It was an amazing point that brought fans leaping to their feet and Pelé jumping for joy into the arms of his teammates. Three to one, Brazil. Thirteen minutes later, it was four to one, Brazil, thanks to a low-dribbling kick by Mario Zagallo.

Agne Simonsson of Sweden tightened the gap soon after by drawing out Brazilian goalkeeper Gilmar and boosting a shot on the unprotected goal. Now there were only ten minutes remaining in the game. If the Swedes were going to tie or overcome their two-point deficit, they would have to move quickly and decisively.

They didn't. Instead, it was Pelé who made the move. In the final moments of World Cup 1958, the seventeen-year-old raced to meet a lobbing pass in front of the goal. The Swedish keeper, Karl Svensson, ran to the same spot, as did two of his teammates. Pelé and one defender reached the ball at nearly the same time. They jumped, heads cocked to intercept the ball.

Pelé got there first. With a solid header, he punched the ball up and over Svensson's reaching arms. The ball took one big hop and then gently bounced into the net. Goal number two for Pelé — and Brazil's first World Cup victory!

Pelé broke down in tears of joy. His teammates boosted him on their shoulders, supporting him as he sagged from sheer exhaustion and overwhelming happiness. The fans, while disappointed that their home team hadn't won, still cheered heartily as the victors grabbed edges of Brazil's flag and ran with it around the pitch. They cheered even louder when the Brazilians honored the host country by exchanging their flag for the Swedish one and running another lap.

And when those fans left the stadium hours later, there was one name on everyone's lips. The name had no real meaning in any language. But for those who spoke the language of soccer, that name soon became synonymous with greatness: Pelé.

⋆ CHAPTER SEVEN ⋆

1962

Twice Is Nice

In the years following his World Cup debut, Pelé continued to amaze crowds with his athleticism, instincts, and winning personality. Soccer fans everywhere couldn't wait to see what he would do when he took to the field for the 1962 tournament in Chile.

They were not disappointed in his performance in Brazil's opening match against Mexico. That game, Pelé scored his team's second goal in the 2–0 victory.

Unfortunately, that was his only point in the tournament. In fact, it was his only full game. Three days later, Brazil faced Czechoslovakia. Early in the match, Pelé suddenly fell, clutching his left thigh. He had torn a muscle and was out for the rest of the Cup.

On that same day, June 2, one of the most vicious soccer games in World Cup history was played. Dubbed the "Battle of Santiago" for the city in which it was held, the match saw players from Chile and Italy coming to blows on the field.

The tension between the two teams had been brewing for weeks. In their newspapers, Italy had branded Chile as a country of illiterate alcoholics. Then Chile had accused Italy of stealing its best players. Animosity grew to a fever pitch, and when the day of the game arrived, the Chilean fans were crying for blood. The Italian players tried to diffuse the situation by throwing roses to the crowd. Their offerings were met with jeers and taunts. And soon after, things went from bad to worse.

From the starting whistle on, players kicked, shoved, and spat at one another. Within minutes, one of Italy's players, Giorgio Ferrini, was ejected for rough tackling. Not long afterward, Chile's Leonel Sánchez threw Umberto Maschio, a native of Argentina, to the ground and punched him in the nose. Sánchez was the son of a boxer and clearly knew how to hit—Maschio's nose was broken.

Amazingly, Sánchez wasn't tossed from the game. But being on the field made him a prime target. A short time later, Mario David avenged his teammate's broken nose with a slashing high kick at Sánchez's throat. The referee blew his whistle; David was ejected.

With the Italian team down two of their starting players, the Chilean squad was able to post two goals in the second half for a 2–0 win. Later, officials said they would have stopped the game to allow players time to cool off but feared that doing so would have caused a riot. "The most stupid, appalling, disgusting, and disgraceful exhibition of football," the British Broadcasting Company called the game.

Meanwhile, other teams were mounting attacks against one another, although they saved their kicks for the ball, not their opponents. But in the semifinal match between Brazil and Chile, blows were exchanged yet again. This time, it was Brazil's star player, Garrincha, whose fists flew in fury.

As a child, Garrincha had suffered a bout of polio, a disease that often leaves victims crippled for life. Garrincha had recovered, but the polio had left him with oddly misshapen legs. Those legs never slowed him down, however. He was one of the sport's best ball handlers and playmakers, a jokester whose humor often relieved his teammates' stress before games.

But Garrincha wasn't laughing when, fed up by the rough handling he was receiving from a Chilean rival, he threw a punch. A fight broke out that ended only when Garrincha was ordered from the field. He left amid a shower of debris from riled-up spectators. Not that his departure changed the outcome of the game; Brazil won, 4–2, to advance to the finals.

The next day, debate swirled over whether Garrincha would be allowed to play in the final match against

Czechoslovakia. Fortunately for his teammates and the Brazilian fans, he was. The South American squad would need every good player it had if it was to be successful against the Czechoslovakians.

Czechoslovakia had clawed its way to the finals with a 1–0 win over Hungary in the quarterfinals and a 3–1 victory against Yugoslavia in the semis. Josef Masopust was their top scorer, but the backbone of their team was their goalkeeper, Vilem Schroif. Schroif had been remarkably effective in the games leading up to the finals. He looked to shut down Brazil's attack.

But Schroif might as well have tried to hold back a flood with a teaspoon. Even without Pelé, the Brazilian offense was packed with talent. While the Czechs surprised everyone by getting on the board first with a sixteenth-minute point by Masopust, the Brazilians powered back with a shot from Pelé's replacement, Amarildo Tavares da Silveira, that squeaked between Schroif and the post to swish into the net.

Amarildo helped his team to their second goal, too, with a blistering pass across the field to teammate José Ely "Zito" de Miranda, who headed the ball into the net. Brazil now had the lead, 2–1.

The late-afternoon sun may have played a part in Brazil's third and final goal. Defender Djalma Santos lobbed a kick in the air toward the goal. It should have been a routine catch for Schroif, but the sun's glare may have blinded him just for a second — long enough for him to lose track of the ball. He bobbled the catch right in front of Vavá, who simply knocked it in for goal number three.

Czechoslovakia couldn't recover. When the game ended twelve minutes later, Brazil had won its second consecutive World Cup!

✶ CHAPTER EIGHT ✶

1966

No Three-peat

In 1966, the World Cup was hosted by soccer's birth-place, England. The country was home to hundreds of thousands of rabid fans who wanted what had so far eluded them in their World Cup appearances: the Jules Rimet Cup.

As was customary, the gold trophy made its way to the host country months before the tournament began. Rather than keeping it under lock and key, the English handlers chose to display it in a London shop window along with a collection of rare stamps. Imagine their horror when one morning they found the window empty!

A frantic search for the iconic Cup turned up nothing at first. In fact, the trophy might never have been found if not for the sharp nose of a little black-and-white dog named Pickles. Pickles and his owner were out for a walk when suddenly the dog started digging at a hedge. When the owner inspected the site, he discovered the trophy, wrapped in newspaper.

He returned it to the proper officials, who no doubt handled it more carefully after that!

In the days leading up to the first match, speculation centered on Brazil's chances of being the first country to "three-peat." Many believed that with Pelé back in the lineup, along with Garrincha and other players from the previous two victories, the defending champions looked good to take the Cup again.

But it was not to be. Targeted from the outset by vicious tackles, the Brazilians were literally knocked out of contention in the first round. Pelé, in particular, had been hacked repeatedly on the field. He was so badly hurt, in fact, that he couldn't play in the second match, which Brazil lost, 3–1, to Hungary.

He was back on the field for game three against Portugal, but as film shows, he again took hit after hit. He left the game, a 3–1 loss, limping and bruised. Disappointed and furious at the brutality, Pelé declared that he would never compete in another World Cup.

"Soccer has been distorted by violence and destructive tactics," he told reporters. "I don't want to end up an invalid."

With Pelé and Brazil out of the picture, all eyes turned to the play of an amazing newcomer from Portugal, twenty-four-year-old Eusébio Ferreira da Silva. His skillful dribbling, combined with his uncanny ability to find the open shot, made him an instant star in soccer-crazed England. With Eusébio leading the charge, the Portuguese reached the quarterfinals.

Portugal's opponent in this round was North Korea. The fact that the North Koreans had made it so far in the tournament came as a surprise to many. They were only in the World Cup because several other nations had dropped out after qualifying. Once in, however, they fought hard to stay in. After falling to the Soviet Union, they tied Chile and then, unbelievably, ousted Italy, 1–0.

The North Koreans looked incredibly strong at the start of their quarterfinal match. In just twenty-five minutes of play, they scored three times!

But then Eusébio took over. Two minutes after North Korea's third point, he boosted the ball into the goal. Two minutes before the break, he hit another. After the half, he made back-to-back penalty kicks — and assisted his teammate José Augusto for the team's fifth goal!

It was goodbye North Korea, hello semifinals for the Portuguese. That was as far as they went, however. Try as they might, they couldn't overcome the onslaught by their English opponents. The star of the show that game was Bobby Charlton, who sent the home fans into a frenzy by scoring both of his team's goals. Eusébio was held to just one, a penalty kick in the final minutes.

While Portugal was falling to England, the Soviet Union was collapsing beneath the powerful play of West Germany. The 1966 World Cup finals would be between the English and the Germans.

The match was played before a sellout crowd at Wembley Stadium in London. The fans buzzed with excitement in the opening minutes—only to fall silent at the twelve-minute mark as Helmut Haller of Germany turned a pass at the right corner of the box into the game's first goal.

Geoff Hurst tied it up soon afterward when he headed a free kick over and past Germany's goal-keeper. The score stayed knotted for the remainder of the first half and far into the second as well. Then, with just thirteen minutes left to play, Martin Peters of England captured the ball near the front of the goal's mouth and converted it into a point with a smashing kick.

The fans went wild. Their screams of joy and encouragement grew louder and louder as the final minutes ticked down. England, birthplace of soccer, was going to win its first World Cup!

Or was it?

Moments before the referee blew his whistle to signal the end of the game, Germany's Wolfgang Weber chased down a loose ball that had rolled free near England's goal. With one swift and decisive blast, he sent it to the back of the net! The score was tied—and the game was forced into extra time.

Those final minutes would yield one of the most controversial plays in World Cup history. Nearly ten minutes in, Hurst snared a cross pass from Alan Ball in front of the German goal. He turned and booted a hard shot. The ball flew through the air, struck the goal's crossbar, and slammed straight down to a point just inside the line.

Goal! The fans and players went insane until—*fweet!* The linesman blew his whistle and rushed forward, arms waving. From his point of view, the ball hadn't struck *behind* the line, but in *front* of it! There was no goal!

The linesman and the referee met on the pitch. As they conferred, soccer fans the world over held their breath. Goal, or no goal?

They got their answer a second later. The officials ruled that the ball had, indeed, hit inside the line. The goal was good! The English were ahead 3–2! And before the extra minutes ended, they were ahead 4–2, thanks to yet *another* goal by the jubilant Hurst. His hat trick was the first, and so far only, ever made during a championship game—and with it, he delivered England's first, and so far only, World Cup victory.

⋆ CHAPTER NINE ⋆

1970

The Return of the King

Pelé was back. After vowing never to play in another World Cup, he had decided to return after all. Key to his decision was a new rule enacted by FIFA.

To address the rough tackling that overshadowed the 1966 World Cup, FIFA established a card system that gave referees the power to first warn, and then eject, any player they caught purposefully attacking an opponent. A yellow card was a warning; a red card was an expulsion.

Amazingly, Pelé's decision to play was almost nullified by Brazil's coach, João Saldanha, who, for some inexplicable reason, cut Pelé from the team! The public outcry against this move was instantaneous — and very, very angry. Pelé was reinstated almost as quickly as Saldanha was replaced. The team's new coach, Mario Zagallo, proved his worth by building one of the best offenses in soccer history. Spearheading that offense was Pelé, the man once declared a national treasure by the Brazilian government.

Brazil coasted through the preliminaries, winning all of its six qualifying matches. The team was equally successful in the first round of group play, going undefeated against Czechoslovakia, Romania, and the defending champion, England. The game against the English was won by a single goal—although it probably would have been a two-goal victory if not for Gordon Banks.

Banks was England's goalkeeper. In the 1966 World Cup, he had prevented teams from Mexico, France, Argentina, and Portugal from scoring a single goal. Only West Germany, in the finals, had managed to get two past him.

He added another goalless game in England's first match of the 1970 Cup by denying Romania. Next up was Brazil.

The Brazilians were fully aware of Banks's abilities. That knowledge may have helped them do what so few others had done: namely, get one past him. The goal was made by Jairzinho, one of Brazil's top players, in the fifty-ninth minute. But it was the goal that *wasn't* made earlier in the game that had fans all over the world cheering.

Brazil was on the attack, rocketing down the field toward Banks. The ball nearly rolled out of bounds but was captured by Jairzinho. He hooked a pass across to the net to Pelé, who was covered by an English defender. Both jumped to intercept. Pelé jumped higher and met the ball with his head.

Banks, meanwhile, leaped into the air, anticipating that the ball would fly high. Instead, the ball shot toward the lower right corner of the net. There was no way Banks should have been able to save it. But he did, somehow twisting his body in midair and stretching just far enough to swat the ball away before it crossed into the net.

"He came from nowhere," a dumbfounded Pelé recalled later. "I was already shouting 'Gooooal!'"

"My first reaction was to look at Pelé," Banks remembered. "He'd ground to a halt. That's all I needed to know."

Behind such stellar play, both Brazil and England made it to the quarterfinals. But that was the end of the road for England, who fell to West Germany in overtime play. The Germans didn't make it farther than the semifinals, however. They were beaten four goals to three in extra minutes by Italy.

That Italy had netted four goals was something of a surprise: the team was known for its defense, not its offense. They would need every defensive trick in the book if they were to win against Brazil, their opponent in the finals.

Pelé drove the front-line force. He scored early in the game with a header off a pass from Roberto Rivelino that caught the Italian goalkeeper napping. Not surprisingly, the Italian team covered the Brazilian superstar with extra care after that, and at the same time they managed to post a goal of their own.

The score was tied at the half, but then the Italians' energy began to flag. Perhaps Mexico's heat or the thin air of the high elevation was getting to them. Or maybe they were simply exhausted from the Brazilians' continuous push.

Whatever the cause, they weren't playing their best in the second half. The Brazilians, on the other hand, were on fire. First Gérson de Oliveira Nunes hit to put Brazil up, 2–1. Then Pelé tricked the Italian goalkeeper with a fake header that turned into a pass to Jairzinho, who converted it into the team's third goal. It was Pelé again with a perfectly aimed pass to team captain Carlos Alberto, who thundered the ball into the net for goal number four.

That shot, ranked among the best ever taken in World Cup history, was the nail in Italy's coffin. When the final seconds ticked away, Brazil had its third World Cup victory! The win had been so decisive that not even the Italian media could find fault. "The best footballers in the world," was what they called the players from South America.

Uruguay in a historic moment: a goal in the first-ever World Cup final match. Uruguay beat Argentina, 4–2.

America's unsung hero, Joe Gaetjens, is hoisted onto his teammates' shoulders after scoring the single goal in the United States' 1–0 win over powerhouse England during the first round of the 1950 World Cup.

Pelé heads in a goal over his Italian rival to put Brazil up 1–0 in the 1970 World Cup final.

Wily Johan Cruyff of the Netherlands avoids Argentina's goalkeeper to score a goal in the 1974 World Cup.

1986: The infamous "Hand of God" goal. Fist raised, Argentina's Diego Maradona (front) literally beats English goalkeeper Peter Shilton to the punch to make one of the most controversial goals in World Cup history.

Brazil's winning goal flies into the net past Italy's goalkeeper in the 1994 World Cup finals, the first to be decided by penalty shoot-out. Brazil won, 3–2, to take its fourth title.

France's Zinedine Zidane seconds before he rockets a penalty kick past Italy's goalkeeper to put his team up 1–0 in the 2006 World Cup final. Later in the game, Zidane was red-carded after headbutting Marco Materazzi.

Brandi Chastain of the United States falls to her knees in celebration after booting in the winning penalty shot for the 1999 World Cup final.

Of those "best footballers," Pelé was the cream of the crop. He was undeniably the most recognizable soccer player in the world, and his jaw-dropping play was matched only by his friendly demeanor on and off the field. Take his reaction to the Gordon Banks save: rather than storming away in frustration as another player might have, Pelé congratulated the goalkeeper with a pat on the back. That same game also saw him exchange jerseys, hugs, and smiles with England's Bobby Moore, a moment caught in a now-famous photograph. Always willing to sign autographs, Pelé was and continues to be the sport's most congenial goodwill ambassador.

But those hoping to catch a glimpse of the superstar in the next World Cup were to be disappointed. The 1970 competition was Pelé's last, although he continued to play for Brazil's Santos team until his retirement in 1974. He relaced his cleats less than a year later, but for a different team and on a different continent. In 1975, he became a member of the New York Cosmos. He played for them until his final game in October of 1977.

Pelé's influence on the world of soccer was singular, but his ability to reach out to his rivals left an even bigger mark. As the Brazilian ambassador to the United Nations once said, "Pelé played football for twenty-two years, and in that time he did more to promote world friendship and fraternity than any other ambassador anywhere."

A British newspaper described him somewhat differently: "How do you spell Pelé? G-O-D."

★ CHAPTER TEN ★

1974

Total Football

The 1974 World Cup competition, held in West Germany, bid goodbye to longtime favorites England and Hungary while welcoming four newcomers: Australia, Haiti, Zaire, and East Germany. It also welcomed a new format for the final stages of play. Rather than single knockout quarterfinals, the eight top teams were separated into two groups, A and B. The four teams within each group played one another, a total of three games apiece, with the best team then advancing on to the final.

The 1974 tournament saw other changes as well. A new solid gold trophy, called simply the World Cup Trophy, replaced the Jules Rimet Trophy, which had been retired by Brazil after its victory in the previous Cup. Taking the helm of FIFA was João Havelange, the first non-European to become president. Also noteworthy was the first red card, given to Chilean player Carlos Caszely for excessive roughness.

But by far the most exciting new development was a style of play known as Total Football.

For years, soccer teams were made up of players who were assigned set positions on the forward line, the midfield, the defensive zone, or the goal. While they could stray from their slots on occasion, mostly they were expected to stay put and cover their territory.

Total Football turned that concept on its head. Now, instead of being pigeonholed in their roles, teammates moved freely among the positions, adapting their play to whatever action unfolded on the field. No position was left uncovered; if a midfielder raced toward the opponent's goal with the ball, for example, his teammates quickly shifted about until his empty position was filled.

Total Football required every player to know how to play every position and how to "read" the field. It demanded that they be flexible, ready to move fluidly into a different spot on the field at a second's notice. In 1974, no player was better at that than Johan Cruyff of the Netherlands.

Cruyff was slim, nimble-footed, and the only soccer player to have a move named after him. The "Cruyff turn," as it is known, is a trick aimed at luring a defender one step out of position. To do the move, the handler controls the ball with his right foot and pretends to move right. When the defender moves with him, the handler then flicks the ball *behind* his own feet—and away from the defender. After that, it's a simple matter of controlling the ball and heading straight for the goal.

Considered one of the sport's top playmakers, Cruyff captured the attention of the world during the 1974 World Cup with his uncanny ability to be in the right place at the right time. Behind his wily expertise and pinpoint accuracy, the Netherlands reached the finals for the first time ever.

There they faced the home team, West Germany, in its first appearance in the finals since its 1966 loss to England. The Germans had won all but one of their opening matches. They lost a politically charged match with East Germany in which the only and winning goal was scored by Jürgen Sparwasser. Still, the West Germans advanced to the second stage of play. There, Yugoslavia and Sweden fell to them by scores of 2–0 and 4–2.

Their third game in this pool was against Poland—and it might as well have taken place *in* a pool, for the pitch was a rain-soaked mess of mud that slowed both sides to a crawl. Neither team scored in the first half; it wasn't until the seventy-sixth minute that the ball found the back of the net. That goal, made by Germany's Gerd Müller, was the only one of the game. Poland was left to battle Brazil for third place, while the West Germans moved on to the finals against the Netherlands.

The final match took place in the Olympiastadion in Munich on July 7. Security at the game—throughout the tournament, in fact—was tighter than it ever had been before, and with good reason.

Two years earlier, Munich had hosted the Summer Olympics. Midway through the competition, a horrifying event took place. Eight Palestinian terrorists took eleven Israeli athletes hostage. They killed two of the hostages and attempted to use the other nine as human shields when they fled the country via airplane. At the airport, the Munich police's rescue efforts went terribly wrong. All the hostages, as well as three terrorists, were killed.

Now, two years later, no one was taking any chances. Security forces, including tanks, were present at airports, and each venue was guarded carefully. Fortunately, the terrible events of 1972 were not repeated at the World Cup.

The battle for the new World Cup Trophy began at four o'clock. Amazingly, one minute after four, the Netherlands scored their first goal! Even more amazingly, West Germany hadn't even touched the ball!

The point came from a penalty kick awarded to the Dutch when Cruyff, dribbling toward the goal, was tackled by Uli Hoeness inside the box. What followed was another World Cup first—the first penalty kick to be taken in a finals match. Johan Neeskens took the kick, calmly booting the ball past goalkeeper Sepp Maier.

Then something curious happened. The Dutch coach Rinus Michels, the man who had developed Total Football for his players, decided to fall back on defense rather than allow his team to put their tried-and-true strategy to work. His decision was based on a desire to protect their one-point lead.

But it backfired. An overzealous sliding tackle by the Netherlands Wim Jansen gave the West Germans a penalty kick of their own. Paul Breitner lined up his shot and trotted forward. Jan Jongbloed, the Dutch goal-keeper, thought Breitner was aiming toward the right side, and so took a side step in that direction. Instead, the kick sent the ball flying toward the lower left corner. Jongbloed was too far out of position to block it.

Tie score, 1–1.

In the minutes remaining in the first half, the two teams fought hard to unravel the knot. Berti Vogts of Germany nearly booted one past Jongbloed, but Jongbloed made the save. Later, Cruyff dished the ball off to teammate Jonny Rep. Rep nearly converted the pass into a goal, but was robbed when Maier stopped the ball.

It wasn't until the forty-third minute that the score changed. Germany's Rainer Bonhof had the ball. He dribbled madly down the right sideline and then angled in toward the goal. He darted around a defender and launched a pass to Müller, who had raced to the front of the goal.

But Müller bobbled the ball! It bounced a few feet behind him. With lightning-quick reflexes, he darted around and snared the loose ball. Then, with a twisting kick, he fired the ball toward the goal — and past Jongbloed!

It was Müller's fourteenth goal of the World Cup, a record at the time. He and his teammates leaped and celebrated on the field. In the stands, the fans went wild. And when neither team scored in the second half, they went even crazier. Twenty years after winning the 1954 World Cup, the West Germans were the champions once more!

Cruyff and his teammates naturally were upset with their performance. "Germany didn't win. We lost it," Cruyff told reporters. Cruyff himself had done all he could, in that game as well as in the preceding matches. In fact, he had a hand — or rather, a foot — in all of the Netherlands' nineteen World Cup goals.

But in the end, his individual performance didn't matter to him. The Cup was in Germany's hands.

★ CHAPTER ELEVEN ★

1978

Working the System?

In 1966, FIFA awarded the host duties for the 1978 World Cup to Argentina. The government immediately went into a frenzy of planning, building, and beautifying their country in anticipation of taking center stage before the world.

What the country's leaders didn't anticipate, however, was that they would be forced from power two years before the tournament took place. The South American country was still struggling to quell civil unrest and uncertainty as the time for the World Cup tournament approached. In light of this, many national teams petitioned for a change to a safer venue.

The requests were denied. Instead, João Havelange worked with the new Argentine government to ensure that the competition would go as smoothly as possible. Luckily, his efforts paid off.

After many months of preliminary rounds, in which a record number of ninety-five teams competed for the fourteen available slots, the 1978 World Cup kicked off on the first of June. All but two of the sixteen teams — Iran and Tunisia — had played in previous tournaments, and three teams, Brazil, West Germany, and Italy, were each returning with more than one championship already under their belts. But this year, the team most people were watching had never won a Cup — although they had come very close four years before.

Behind its innovative "Total Football" strategy, the team from the Netherlands had rocketed through the qualifiers, winning five of its six matches. In the course of those games, the Dutch booted in eleven goals while giving up only three. Many expected them to repeat their previous World Cup efforts and go all the way to the finals.

And that's just what they did, although they didn't get there as easily as some thought they would. After dumping Iran, 3–0, in their first game, they found themselves locked in a tie with the determined and surprisingly strong team from Peru — and then on the wrong side of a 3–2 score in a game against Scotland. Instead of a commanding first-place rank at the end of the first round, the Netherlands wound up in second.

That placing might have been just the wake-up call the Dutch players needed. After their lackluster showing in the openers, they thumped Austria, 5–1; tied the 1974 West German champs, 2–2; and won a hard-fought battle against Italy, 2–1. Those scores were good enough to see them through to the finals.

Meanwhile, Argentina was busy slicing its way past its opponents to reach its first finals in nearly half a century. On the way there, the team may have received a boost that, while not illegal, had fans from rival Brazil crying foul.

Brazil, Argentina, Poland, and Peru were put together in Group B for the second stage of play. The winner of this stage would advance to the finals. On June 14, Brazil beat Peru, 3–0. Two and a half hours later, Argentina beat Poland, 2–0. Four days later, Poland beat Peru, knocking that nation out of contention. Meanwhile, Brazil and Argentina ended their match in a 0–0 draw.

There were now two games left to go in the round. First up was Brazil against Poland. Brazil won, 3–1, thus assuring them second place in Group B at the very least. If Argentina should lose or tie in its upcoming match with Peru, Brazil would go on to the finals. Even if Argentina won, Brazil had a chance of advancing: if its total goals for the round were greater than Argentina's, Brazil would be declared the round's overall victor.

This is when things got interesting. According to

rumors, the Peruvians didn't want the Brazilians to advance. Peru's goalkeeper had a particular reason for wanting Argentina to succeed—he was a native-born Argentine. Some believed he feared that if he prevented Argentina from scoring, then his country of birth would hate him forever.

Whether the rumors were true or not, the results remained the same. The team from Peru gave up two goals in the first half and then four more in the second. Those six unanswered goals were enough to push Argentina into the finals—and leave the Brazilians seething at the injustice of the schedule. After all, if the Peruvians hadn't known the results of the Brazil–Poland match, they wouldn't have known how many goals Argentina needed to win the finals slot. Without that knowledge they might have played harder, perhaps even unseated the Argentines.

But Brazil's protests fell on deaf ears, for the time being anyway.

The final match between the Netherlands and the host country was scheduled to be played at three o'clock on June 25. A crowd of nearly seventy-two thousand rabid soccer fans filled the stands hours before. As the time drew near, they grew more and more excited. Then at last, the locker room doors opened and out came the Dutch players resplendent in their electric-orange jerseys.

But where were the Argentine players? Usually, both teams filed onto the field side by side. This year, however, Argentina's coach, César Luis Menotti, had decided to psych out the rival squad. He kept the Dutch waiting on the field for ten minutes; with each minute that ticked by, the Dutch became more and more agitated. They had hit the pitch charged up and ready to play, but now that energy was turning sour!

Menotti's tactic had only a temporary affect on the Dutch players, however. Once the game began, they settled down and found their rhythm. So did the Argentines. The first half saw both launching attack after attack. Both threatened to get on the board first, yet after more than thirty minutes, the game was still scoreless.

Then, in the thirty-eighth minute, hometown hero Mario Kempes took control. Kempes had starred in earlier wins by Argentina, scoring four of his team's eight goals in the second stage of play. Now he thrilled spectators by collecting a pass from Leopoldo Luque and drilling it across the confetti-covered pitch and into the net.

The score remained at Argentina 1, Netherlands 0, throughout the first half. After the break, the Dutch pushed even harder than before, yet time and again failed to get one by the Argentine goalkeeper. It wasn't until eight minutes before the end of the game that they finally managed to tie things up with a spectacular header by Dick Nanninga.

The battle raged on through the final minutes of regulation play with neither team adding to their score. The game would be decided in overtime.

While no game is ever won by a single player, it can be argued that one man made the difference for his team in this final. In the one hundred and fifth minute, Mario Kempes danced through a sea of defenders toward the goal. Jongbloed charged out and stopped Kempes's kick—only to watch in horror as Kempes darted around him and nudged the ball into the net!

And Kempes wasn't finished. As the one hundred and fifteenth minute approached, he found team-mate Daniel Bertoni with a pass. Bertoni caught it cleanly and launched the ball across the box and into the goal.

The Argentine fans—loud, raucous, and excited throughout the match—went into a frenzy. The celebrations lasted for days afterward. At long last, Argentina was the champion of the soccer world.

✯ CHAPTER TWELVE ✯

1982

Bigger than Ever

Twenty-four. That was how many nations would participate in the World Cup's newly expanded format. Soccer had grown so popular in so many parts of the globe that sixteen slots were simply not enough anymore. Those twenty-four teams were separated into six groups of four for first-round play. While many of the matches ended predictably, there were some surprising upsets.

The most stunning of these was the 2–1 defeat of West Germany by newcomer Algeria. The Germans recovered from the loss to beat Chile, 4–1, in their next match. The Algerians, meanwhile, lost to Austria, 2–0, and then beat Chile, 3–2. Chile was out, having lost to Austria earlier in the series, 1–0.

There was just one game left in the series, that between West Germany and Austria. The question now was, how would the remaining teams rank when that game was finished?

The answer would be decided in the final point

tally. Algeria had earned five goals while giving up five. Before the match, West Germany also had earned five goals, but only let in three. Austria had scored three goals and allowed none.

From these statistics, it would seem that Algeria would beat out Austria for second place unless Austria won against West Germany. But two of Algeria's goals had been earned during its "away" game against Germany. In the final tally, those two would count for just a little less than goals made during "home" games.

Both West Germany and Austria knew that going into the final match of their group play. They knew something else, too: if Germany won by a score of 1–0, then it would take first place in the group — and Austria, having given up just one away goal to Algeria's two, would take second.

With that in mind, the Austrians agreed to oust the Algerians by allowing the Germans to score the single necessary goal. That goal was scored ten minutes into the game. After that, both the Germans and the Austrians treated the match like a practice, pushing the ball this way and that while never really attempting to score.

The Algerians realized what was happening, of course. Like the Brazilians in the previous Cup, they cried foul. But there was nothing anyone could do at that point. FIFA eventually changed the scheduling of group play so that in future World Cups, games would be played at the same time. No team would ever again go into a final match knowing how many points they needed to advance.

Final score: West Germany 1, Austria 0 — and goodbye, Algeria.

The Algerians were partly avenged in the second-round play when the Austrians came in behind the French and were thus eliminated from the semifinals. Germany managed to stay alive, however, squeaking out a 2–1 win over Spain and ending their match against England in a 0–0 draw.

Also reaching the semifinals were Poland and Italy. These two teams had met earlier in the tournament in a game that had ended in a scoreless tie. That they were to meet again now was something of a shock, for most had believed Italy would be eliminated in the second round by Brazil. But in one of the most amazing upsets of the competition, Italy won, 3–2, beating a team laden with talent. Even more amazing, all three of Italy's goals were scored by one player, Paolo Rossi.

Rossi was a talented player with a checkered soccer history. After a promising debut, he suffered from knee problems and was let go by his team, Juventus. He recovered, however, and grew into a capable player who often slammed home big goals. Although not a standout then, he helped Italy to the World Cup in 1978. Soon afterward, trouble found him again. He and several other players were accused of fixing matches. Rossi was never found guilty, but he was suspended from soccer for two years nonetheless. He came back just in time to take part in the 1982 World Cup.

His return to the international tournament had many people muttering in dismay. Rossi may have been good once, but now?

Rossi turned those mutters into cheers in the second-round Brazil–Italy match. He scored five minutes into that game. Twenty minutes later, he broke a tie to give Italy a one-goal advantage. And in the seventy-fourth minute, he broke a *second* tie to give Italy the win!

That victory was by far Italy's most electrifying. And Rossi wasn't done yet. He scored both of Italy's goals in its 2–0 win over Poland, earning his team a shot at the championship title!

To get that title, Italy would have to beat West Germany. The Germans weren't about to go down without a fight, as they'd shown in their semifinal match against France; that game left one French player unconscious when the German goalkeeper plowed into him. It was also the first semifinal to be decided by a penalty shoot-out. Germany managed to put one goal more into the net than France to take its place on the pitch with Italy.

Italy entered the finals as the crowd favorites. Germany, on the other hand, found itself the object of jeers from people who felt the team had cheated Algeria in the earlier round. Perhaps the negative vibe affected the Germans, or maybe they were still exhausted from the grueling game against France.

Whatever the cause, Germany simply couldn't hold its own against the Italian attack. The first half ended without a score. Then at the start of the second, Rossi plugged one into the net, his sixth consecutive goal and the team's first of the game. Twelve minutes later, teammate Marco Tardelli booted in the second. When Alessandro Altobelli blasted in a third, the game was in Italy's pocket.

Not even a late-game goal by Paul Breitner could dampen the Italians' enthusiasm. Tardelli summed up his teammates' joy with a wild, fist-pumping romp around the pitch. With that victory, Italy joined Brazil as the second team to win three championships!

⋆ CHAPTER THIRTEEN ⋆

1986

"The Hand of God"

The thirteenth World Cup tournament almost didn't have a host. Colombia had originally been selected, but two years before the competition was to begin, the government announced that it didn't have the money to foot the bills. The United States, Canada, and Mexico all put in bids to take Colombia's place. Mexico won, becoming the first country to host two World Cups.

Natural disaster nearly prevented them from assuming that role, however. On September 19, 1985, residents of Mexico City were shaken from their beds by a devastating earthquake. Buildings collapsed, leaving thousands dead and hundreds of thousands homeless. Pipes that transported drinking water were in disrepair for weeks. Electricity, communications, transportation, and other services were also cut off. Hospitals were overrun with wounded.

Amazingly, the stadiums dotting the surrounding areas were unaffected. When FIFA contacted

Mexico's government with an offer to find a new host country, the authorities insisted that they could—and would—fulfill their role. Not to do so would be a further blow to their country's shattered morale.

In May, the twenty-four national teams that had made it to the final competition arrived in Mexico for the first round of games. The format had changed slightly from previous years; this time, the top two teams from the initial six groups would be joined by the top four third-place finishers for a sixteen-game knockout round. The surviving eight teams would then take part in the quarterfinals, with the four winners of that round advancing to the semifinals. As always, the two victors of the semifinals would then face off for the championship title.

There were three newcomers to the Cup in 1986: Canada, Iraq, and Denmark. The last of these proved to be one of the most surprising teams of the first round. Grouped with Uruguay, Scotland, and West Germany, the plucky players from the tiny Scandinavian country went undefeated to earn a spot in the round of sixteen! Their biggest win came against Uruguay; in the second half, they plugged four goals into the net for a game total of six. Preben Elkjaer was responsible for three of those goals, his team's first World Cup hat trick. Uruguay, two-time world champion, scored just once.

The knockout round was as far as the aptly nick-named "Danish Dynamite" got, however. Spain trounced them, 5–1. But Denmark's meteoric rise proved once again that every team in the World Cup has a shot at the prize.

Morocco discovered just that. Like Denmark, Mo-rocco was the unexpected survivor of the first round and, in doing so, became the first African country ever to advance in the competition. Unfortunately, its ride ended with a loss to West Germany, 1–0.

The round of sixteen produced some unforeseen upsets, too. Belgium outlasted the Soviet Union's one-man onslaught, a hat trick by Igor Belanov, to win in extra minutes, 4–3. France unseated the reigning champs from Italy, 2–0. And things got ugly in the Argentina–Uruguay match, with seven players receiving cautions. Luckily for the Argentines, their star player was not among those carded.

Diego Maradona had been playing soccer all his life. Too young to be part of the national team for the 1978 World Cup, he was added to the squad for the 1982 competition in Spain. There he booted in two goals in first-round games before his hot temper got him ejected for roughing up a Brazilian player. Now, in 1986, he was determined to show the world what he could do.

His first contribution to Argentina's bid for the

finals came in the second game, when he booted in a goal against the Italians to tie the match, 1–1. He nearly added a second goal to his personal tally in the knockout game against Uruguay, but officials disallowed the point. Luckily, one of his teammates had put one in the net, so Argentina survived and continued on to the quarterfinals.

It was in this match, against England, that Maradona made two goals that have gone down in soccer history. Six minutes into the second half, English defender Steve Hodge lofted the ball into the air in an attempted pass to his goalkeeper, Peter Shilton. Shilton ran to make the catch, arms outstretched high over his head.

At the same time, Maradona raced to meet the ball. He, too, leaped high in the air, raising one arm as he did. It seemed unlikely that the Argentine would out-jump the Englishman—after all, Maradona stood at just five feet five inches while Shilton was over six feet tall. But somehow, Maradona connected instead of Shilton. As the two players fell in a heap, the ball bounded into the net for Argentina's first goal!

Maradona leaped to his feet, shouting and celebrating. But interestingly, none of his teammates ran to celebrate with him right away. Film of the play shows the reason for their hesitation. Maradona had punched the ball into the net with his fist!

Maradona knew that the official had missed his flagrant foul. With no instant replay at the time, he realized there was just one thing to do.

"Come hug me," he recalled yelling to his teammates, "or the referee isn't going to allow it!" Only then did the celebration take place for the goal Maradona later dubbed "the Hand of God."

England must have been seething at the mistakenly awarded point. But there was no mistaking the goal that happened next.

Just three minutes after the Hand of God, Maradona received a pass from Héctor Enrique. He was just shy of the half-field mark. Three English defenders moved in—only to find that Maradona was no longer there.

Legs flashing, the Argentine raced down the field with the English players in hot pursuit. Two converged on him, but he threaded his way between them as if they were no more than orange cones set up for dribbling practice. He then cut toward the goal. Shilton came out to challenge him, but Maradona was simply unstoppable. With one swift and decisive kick, he launched the ball into the net. Goal!

The entire ten-second run displayed Maradona's incredible ability to outthink and outmaneuver his defenders. It is considered by many soccer followers to be the best goal ever made in the World Cup. That day, it was good enough to clinch Argentina's victory over England.

Argentina continued its run for the championship in the semifinals, where Maradona and his teammates dominated Belgium. While Belgium took more shots on goal overall, none of them managed to find the back of the net. Maradona, on the other hand, walloped back-to-back goals in the first ten minutes of the second half. That's all his team needed. Final score: Argentina 2, Belgium 0.

The South American nation was back in the finals for the third time in World Cup history. Its opponent, West Germany, was making its fifth appearance there. Both teams were packed with talent, but it was Argentina who landed the first blow.

Maradona, the obvious scoring threat, was being closely guarded. That left his teammate José Luis Brown wide open — and Brown took full advantage by heading a free kick over the German goalkeeper for the first point of the game.

The second point belonged to Argentina, too. This time it was Jorge Valdano who charged virtually unchallenged into the penalty box. One kick later, Argentina led, 2–0.

But the Germans hadn't reached the finals by lying down and playing dead. They rallied late in the second half and socked in back-to-back goals in just sixteen minutes. As the clock ticked down, the match looked poised to go into extra time.

It didn't, thanks to Maradona. With just seven minutes remaining in the final, he captured the ball in the midst of a swarm of German players and made a jaw-dropping pass to teammate Jorge Burruchaga. Seconds later, Burruchaga scored! And when Argentina held on to their 3–2 lead, they had their second World Cup trophy.

⋆ CHAPTER FOURTEEN ⋆

1990

An Empty Cup

By all accounts, the 1990 World Cup in Italy was the worst ever played. It was low scoring, with an average of fewer than three goals per game. Matches featured defensive "strategy" that recalled the days when Pelé was mauled on the pitch. Brutal hacks, vicious attacks, and slashing tackles resulted in a record sixteen red cards. With so much of the focus on defense, many games ended in draws; four of the twelve games in the final rounds were decided by penalty shoot-outs. Perhaps most telling of all, the second-place team scored just five goals on the way to the championship!

Fortunately, there were a few high points that lifted the competition out of the doldrums. Cameroon, a small African nation, proved the most inspiring—and one of its players, Roger Milla, became a fan favorite.

Milla wasn't originally slated to play for Cameroon. At thirty-eight, he was considered to be past his prime, at least by Cameroon's coach. The president of Cameroon disagreed. He insisted that Milla be added to the roster, for he believed Milla could provide the spark the team needed to succeed.

As it turned out, the president was right: Milla had plenty of life still in him. While he wasn't a starter, he netted several key goals coming off the bench. After watching his teammates beat the reigning champs, Argentina, in the first match, 1–0, he stuck two goals in during a hard-fought victory over Romania. He chalked up two lifesavers in the knockout round of sixteen, handing Cameroon a 2–1 victory over Colombia and a place in the quarterfinals — the first time an African nation had advanced that far.

But the quarterfinals were the end of the line for the sentimental favorites, unfortunately. After holding their own against England throughout regulation play, they lost, 3–2, in extra minutes when Gary Lineker blasted two penalty kicks past Cameroon's goalkeeper.

Penalty kicks made the difference for Argentina late in the competition, too. But it was an astonishing pass by the previous Cup's top player, Maradona, that boosted Argentina past the round of sixteen.

The match was against Brazil. Once known for its brilliant offense, Brazil had reworked its lineup in recent months to favor defense. There were now fewer players on the front line and a sweeper whose chief duty was to help protect the goal. Pelé, who was in the stands, remarked that, in his opinion, the new lineup was doomed to failure.

He was right. Brazil's concentration on defense left it weak offensively. And when its defense broke down, it was rendered powerless. That's what happened late in the game against Argentina. Scoreless through the eightieth minute, Maradona wove effortlessly through a sea of hapless defenders and sent a brilliant pass to teammate Claudio Caniggia. Caniggia was all alone; one kick later, the Argentines were up, 1–0. Ten minutes after that, they were on their way to the quarterfinals—and one week and two victories after *that,* the team reached the finals for the second time in a row.

Along the way, Argentina literally thrashed the host country, Italy, in one of the most physical contests of the competition. Three Argentine players were given red cards for their abusive play. Incensed at seeing their players treated this way, many Italian spectators jeered and hurled objects at the Argentines when they entered the stadium for the finals against West Germany.

Such obvious disapproval of their tactics didn't stop Argentina from playing rough, however. In fact, one of their players, Pedro Monzón, earned the dubious honor of becoming the first to be tossed out of a World Cup final for his behavior. His teammate Gustavo Dezotti joined him later in the game after grabbing a West German player by the throat.

But by then, the match had already been decided. Not surprisingly, the single goal of the game was a penalty kick awarded after a foul by Argentina. Andreas Brehme took the shot, which sailed past the Argentine goalkeeper's hands. With that kick, West Germany recaptured the crown it had last worn in 1974.

⋆ CHAPTER FIFTEEN ⋆

1994

A Shoot-out – and a Shooting

Since the first World Cup in 1930, soccer had grown into the number one sport on the planet. Its popularity outshone every other competitive game wherever it was played—with one notable exception.

For some reason, the United States had failed to give soccer a proper home. While other sports such as baseball, basketball, football, and ice hockey all had successful professional leagues, soccer did not. It wasn't that citizens didn't have access to soccer; in fact, with each passing year more and more children, teenagers, and adults were joining hometown teams. Creating a league from such a solid base should have been simple.

Instead, it took a push from FIFA for the U.S. to finally launch its own network of professional squads. When the United States put in a bid to host the 1994 World Cup, FIFA accepted, but on one condition: it had to develop a professional soccer league. The

United States agreed, and two years after hosting the 1994 Cup, Major League Soccer was born.

The opening rounds of the 1994 World Cup began on June 17. Football stadiums from Foxboro, Massachusetts, to Pasadena, California, opened their gates wide, treating foreign visitors as honored guests. Contrary to what many other nations feared, these venues were packed to capacity every game with cheering American fans.

These fans were rewarded with a style of play that was much improved over the one seen at the previous low-scoring, viciously defensive tournament. After 1990, FIFA passed rules aimed at encouraging players to score goals. To that end, winning teams in the first round would now be awarded three points instead of two. This extra point meant that players would be rewarded for trying to win rather than trying not to lose, or simply holding the game at a tie.

FIFA also decided it was time to end a very dangerous move, the from-behind tackle. Too many players had been badly injured in the previous Cup to let such a practice continue. Now anyone caught tackling from behind would be ejected.

Another rule change was directed at keeping the play moving. Before, goalkeepers were permitted to pick up a ball passed to them by a defender, bounce it a few times, and then boot it back into play. Now, they could only handle passes from teammates with their feet. If they didn't get rid of the ball quickly, a wily attacker could swoop in for the kill.

And finally, FIFA eased up on the controversial offside rule. Attackers would now be given the benefit of the doubt in a potential offside situation.

"When in doubt, keep the flag down" was FIFA's new direction to referees.

The rule changes were greeted with enthusiasm by soccer followers, including Pelé. "No doubt we will see more goals this time," he promised reporters.

Truer words were never spoken. The first round of matches had a huge jump in scores. One game saw a World Cup first when Oleg Salenko of Russia laid five of his team's six goals into the net!

That same match yielded another record, too. Crowd favorite Roger Milla, now forty-two years, one month, and eight days old, showed that he hadn't slowed down one bit in the past four years. He made Cameroon's only goal to become the oldest player in Cup history to score.

Other players drew just as much applause from the enthusiastic fans. Italian Roberto Baggio, also known as "the Divine Ponytail," gave thrilling performances throughout the early round. But it was his second-to-last-minute goal and overtime penalty kick in the knockout game win over Nigeria that earned him a place in the hearts of thousands. Hristo Stoich-kov of Bulgaria was equally astonishing. Behind his goal-scoring attacks, his team went all the way to the semifinals.

Two other players made headlines too, but not for their outstanding play. After years in the limelight as Argentina's soccer hero, Diego Maradona was sent packing when he tested positive for banned drugs. Suspicion fell on him after he went into a crazed cel-ebratory dance after a goal in the first game. Mara-dona had been caught using before but allowed back in. This time he was gone for good.

The other player's story was much more tragic. In an early game against the United States, Colombian defender Andrés Escobar made a terrible mistake — he scored an "own goal," accidentally kicking the ball past his teammate and into the net. When the game ended in a 2–1 loss, Colombia was out of the tourna-ment. Ten days later, the disgraced Escobar was shot to death outside a nightclub in Colombia by a man allegedly enraged by the own goal.

Amid such tragedies, the Cup marched on. The U.S. team managed to stay alive into the second round, where they played Brazil. Given the difference in the two countries' soccer history — Brazil was soccer mad, the U.S. just beginning to catch the fever — few gave the North Americans much of a chance. Some even predicted the Brazilians would be able to score at will against the less experienced host team.

That didn't happen, although the Brazilians certainly tried their best to make those predictions come true. They attacked over and over, forcing the United States' players to fall back on defense and completely neglect their offense. In fact, the records show that they didn't attempt a single shot!

Despite the Brazilian onslaught, the game was scoreless for the first seventy-four minutes. Then, to the Brazilian fans' great relief, José Roberto Gama de Oliveira, known as Bebeto, finally pushed one past the U.S. goalkeeper. The South Americans walked away with the win, although chances are they didn't feel like celebrating. After all, they had botched all but one scoring opportunity against a much weaker team.

Brazil was the only team from the Americas to reach the quarterfinals. The other seven were all from Europe. But anyone who predicted a European-only final was mistaken. Brazil beat the Netherlands and then Sweden to reach the championship round for the fifth time.

Facing Brazil on the pitch was the powerful team from Italy. With each country owning three world championships, it looked to be a match for the ages.

It wasn't. After ninety minutes of regulation play,

neither team had scored. The game was still dead-locked at 0–0 after extra time. For the first time ever, the World Cup would be decided by penalty shoot-out.

Five players from each team were selected to kick. Italy, the away team, went first for the series of alternating shots. Eight shots later, the tally stood at Brazil 3, Italy 2.

Roberto Baggio, his leg bandaged because of a hamstring pull, went to the line for Italy. If his kick was good, the score would be tied, but Brazil would still have one final chance to go ahead. If he missed, however, the Brazilians would win without having to take their last shot.

Baggio trotted forward, accelerating as he approached the ball. He drew his foot back and kicked. The ball soared high — too high! It flew over the goal's crossbar and into the field beyond!

Twenty-four years after its last victory, Brazil was once more on top of the world.

✴ CHAPTER SIXTEEN ✴

1998

Host Heroes

It may seem surprising that, given the number of nations in the world who vie to take part in the World Cup, many of the same countries wind up hosting the tournament over and over. But the truth is, the World Cup, like the Olympics, can be very expensive to hold. Money must be spent on promotion, on upgrading venues, on television and media coverage, and on making sure that the millions of visitors the event attracts can be housed, fed, and transported comfortably.

Still, it is an honor to host, and in 1998, that honor belonged to Jules Rimet's birthplace, France. World Cup spectators would be coming from more countries than ever before as the format had undergone yet another expansion. Thirty-two teams from the six continental zones would now have a chance at the ultimate prize.

As before, the teams were divided into groups of four (originally A–F, now A–H). But instead of the top two teams plus the best of the third-place ranks advancing to the knockout round of sixteen, only the top two from each group would move forward. After that, everything remained the same — quarterfinals to semifinals to finals.

There were a few surprises in the first round, such as the strong showing by newcomer Croatia, but even more disappointments. Spain had hoped to go at least as far as the knockout, but instead fell victim to an early slump and ended up losing in the first round. Team U.S.A. lost all three of its matches to come in dead last in its group. Cameroon, so strong in the previous two Cups, also failed to advance.

Another disappointment was England. The English players came in a close second place behind Romania in their group and hoped to overcome Argentina in the round of sixteen. But it was not to be, although they didn't go down without a fight. In the first half of the match, each team scored on penalty kicks. The tie was unraveled by a fabulous goal by England's Michael Owen. Taking a pass just over the midfield line, he raced down the field, dodged four defenders, and walloped the ball into the net.

"Splendida goal! Splendida goal!" one announcer raved.

Unfortunately, later in the match, Owen's teammate and international superstar David Beckham was sent off for kicking Argentina's Diego Simeone. One player down, England gave up a goal—and when the game went into a penalty shoot-out, they felt Beckham's absence even more, failing to convert on two of their five chances. Argentina made four to go on in the competition.

Meanwhile, to the great excitement of the home crowd, France was posting its best showing in years. They tied with Argentina for the greatest number of goals scored in the first round, and then beat Paraguay in extra minutes to reach the quarterfinals. There they knocked out Italy in yet another shoot-out to move ahead to the semifinals.

Their opponents there were the Croatians, who had amazed spectators by coming out on top against Romania and Germany. They fought hard against France, too, but this time ended on the wrong side of a 2–1 score. The host country had reached the finals!

Facing France was Brazil, the defending champion and holder of four World Cup Trophies. Eighty thousand adoring fans crammed into the Stade de France in Saint-Denis knowing that, whatever the outcome, they were going to witness soccer history. If Brazil won, they would vault to the top of the international competition as five-time champions. If France won, it would be their first victory. Either way, the match promised to be lively and exciting.

It was—for the French, anyway. Their star player, Zinedine "Zizou" Zidane, led the charge. At the twenty-seven-minute mark, he leaped above Brazil's defenders and headed a corner kick into the net. He repeated the effort less than twenty minutes later, converting another corner kick from the opposite side of the goal with another header. But it was the final goal, made by Emmanuel Petit in the very last seconds, that sent the crowd into a frenzy of joy—for it sealed Brazil's fate once and for all.

France, birthplace of soccer's greatest champion and World Cup pioneer, Jules Rimet, had finally earned the sport's highest award.

✶ CHAPTER SEVENTEEN ✶

2002

Five-time Champs

The 2002 World Cup marked a break with tradition. For the first time ever, the competition was not held in either a European or an American nation, but rather in Asia. And, for the first time ever, it was cohosted by two countries, South Korea and Japan. This joint effort meant that three slots of the thirty-two openings were already filled, although due to a rule change, this would be the last time the defending champions were automatically given a slot in the Cup.

That left 29 spots available to the 193 nations taking part in the qualifying rounds. Twenty-five of those nearly two hundred entrants were taking part in the competition for the first time; four of them—China, Ecuador, Slovenia, and Senegal—would reach the World Cup itself. Among the other nations participating were all seven previous Cup winners: England, Argentina, Germany, Brazil, France, Italy, and Uruguay.

Soccer followers buzzed with anticipation, wondering which, if any, of these seven would add another trophy to its shelf.

It wouldn't be France. With their best player, Zinedine Zidane, sidelined with a leg injury, the one-time champs bowed out in the first round after losing to Senegal and Denmark and ending their match against Uruguay in a draw.

That draw didn't help Uruguay too much, however. Those players, too, fell to Senegal and Denmark. They managed to place third in their group, but only because they scored goals during their matches — something France, unbelievably, didn't do even once!

The rise of Senegal was one of the big stories of the early round. The "Lions of Teranga," as they were nicknamed, roared their way past Sweden in the round of sixteen to reach the quarterfinals. Henri Camara was the hero of that game, scoring the African nation's first goal in the thirty-seventh minute for a 1–1 tie and then draining the winning shot in extra time for the 2–1 win. Unfortunately for Senegal fans, the tables were turned in their next match when they lost to Turkey by a single goal after extra time.

The most exciting games of the first round were played in Group F. This foursome was dubbed the "Group of Death" because the teams — Argentina,

England, Nigeria, and Sweden—were all equally talented. Only two could survive the first stage, however, and after the six games those two were Sweden and England. One of the sport's most recognizable figures, David Beckham, was the hero in England's defeat of rival Argentina. He booted in the only goal of the game, a beautiful penalty shot at the forty-fourth-minute mark.

Argentina's failure meant only four previous Cup holders, Germany, Italy, Brazil, and England, were left. But would any make it through the round of sixteen?

It was a close call for Germany, who needed eighty-eight minutes to score the game's one and only goal against the surprisingly strong underdog Paraguay. England won that same day, 3–0, over Denmark. Brazil kept its head above water in its match against Belgium with a 2–0 victory. Italy wasn't as fortunate. After scoring a fast goal in its knockout game against South Korea, the three-time champs couldn't hold the host country at bay. With just two minutes left, the Koreans tied the game and then took the win in extra time.

One down, three remaining. But would all three stay alive in the quarterfinals? Not a chance, simply because England and Brazil were pitted against each other in the first game. There could be just one winner, and that day belonged to Brazil.

The match started well for England. Midway through the first half, Michael Owen sprinted free down the left side of the pitch, received a cross pass from Emile Heskey, and outran Brazilian defender Lucio. Five steps later, he blasted the ball into the net past goalkeeper Marcos.

Brazil tied the game twenty minutes later, and then jumped into the lead at the fifty-minute mark. England couldn't recover. Brazil 2, England 1; England out, Brazil on to the semifinals!

Germany joined Brazil in the semifinal round by beating the unexpectedly strong team from the United States in a close 1–0 match. Turkey continued its journey as well by defeating Senegal. South Korea sent its citizens into paroxysms of joy with its penalty shoot-out victory over Spain. That Turkey and South Korea had lasted so long in the tournament amazed many soccer followers. The question now was, how would they fare against powerhouses Germany and Brazil?

Better than anticipated, was the answer. Korea faced Germany in the first game. It was a defensive duel from the outset, with neither team scoring in the first seventy-four minutes. Then Oliver Neuville got the ball and streaked down the sideline. Teammate Oliver Bierhoff ran parallel down the middle, looking for a pass. When it came, however, it was just behind him. He turned to chase it—only to find his teammate

Michael Ballack already there. With a massive kick, Ballack sent the ball rocketing into the net. Goal!

The game ended fifteen minutes later after neither team scored again. Germany was through to the finals for the seventh time in World Cup history!

There Germany would face its longtime rival, Brazil, who had set aside Turkey, 1–0. The single goal had come from the foot of Ronaldo Luis Nazário de Lima. This was the third World Cup appearance for Ronaldo (not to be confused with his teammate Ronaldo de Assis Moreira, also known as Ronaldinho or Ronaldo Gaúcho).

Ronaldo had been a member of Brazil's team in 1994 at seventeen but did not play. In the 1998 competition, he seemed poised for greatness. Leading into Brazil's run to the finals, he had booted in four goals and one penalty shot. Then, hours before the deciding match was to begin, something happened: Ronaldo's name was removed from Brazil's starting lineup. Even more mysteriously, it was added again just half an hour before the kickoff!

What was going on? Rumors about the star player buzzed through the soccer world. It was only much later that the truth came out.

According to his roommate, Roberto Carlos, Ronaldo had suffered a seizure some time in the night. He was rushed to the hospital, where he underwent several physical and neurological tests. All came back with reports that he was fine.

Ronaldo declared he had no memory of what happened. He also declared himself perfectly fit and eager to play in the final. But it was clear to most that the previous night's events had taken their toll, for he played a sluggish game that ended in Brazil's defeat by the French.

The press was not kind to Ronaldo in the years that followed. He suffered knee injuries as well, leading some to whisper that he was done. But he refused to give up. He worked his way back to health and onto the national team. It remained to be seen if he could work his way back into the hearts of Brazilians.

It didn't take long for him to do just that. In Brazil's quest for the crown, he posted five goals. In the semifinals, he added a sixth with a forty-ninth-minute blast just inside the penalty box.

"Oh, what do you say about that? Extraordinary!" a British announcer cried after the ball bounced into the net. "Every World Cup needs a hero and Ronaldo is one here!"

Brazil won — and the next day, Ronaldo was a hero again.

The game with Germany was played before a sell-out crowd in Yokohama, Japan. Partway through the first half, Ronaldo threatened with a point-blank shot on Germany's outstanding goalkeeper, Oliver Kahn. To his and everybody else's shock, the kick flew wide. But the attempt had a lasting effect nonetheless, for it sparked Brazil to step up its attacks.

Kahn was too masterful for them, however—at least until the sixty-seventh minute. Then he bobbled what should have been a routine catch. That was all Ronaldo needed. Flying forward, he snared the free ball on his foot and kicked. Kahn made a desperate lunge from the ground, but he just couldn't get in front of it. Brazil was on the board, 1–0.

Twelve minutes later, that score had changed to 2–0. Again, Ronaldo made the shot, although much of the credit must go to his teammate Rivaldo, who faked a stop before letting the ball continue on to Ronaldo—who then blasted it into the net.

The Germans simply couldn't recover in the time that remained. When the final seconds ticked off the clock, Brazil had won its fifth title, the most of any country in the world!

"It is a wonderful feeling to have won this trophy," a joyful Ronaldo told *FIFA Magazine* soon after the win. "I used to visualize the trophy in front of my eyes and imagine what a wonderful feeling it must be to hold it up in the air. It was a fabulous feeling actually to hold it in my hands."

CHAPTER EIGHTEEN

2006

The Header That Shocked the World

One billion. That's how many people were expected to watch the 2006 World Cup final. If only Jules Rimet could have seen just how far soccer had come!

The road to that final game was littered with fallen favorites. While Ronaldo returned in fine form, earning a place in the books by besting Gerd Müller's long-standing record of fourteen World Cup goals, he could not get Brazil into the finals. The South Americans were unseated by France in the quarterfinals by a single goal made by standout Thierry Henry.

Argentina was thwarted in the quarterfinal round, too, in a 4–2 penalty shoot-out won by Germany. England, likewise, was shunted aside in this round by a shoot-out, which yielded Portugal three goals to England's two.

Of the greats, only host country Germany, three-time champs Italy, and recent winners France lived up to expectations by reaching the semifinals. And then, following Germany's defeat by the Italians, there were just two.

Italy's journey to the finals had been nearly flawless, with just two goals scored against them. One of those was an "own goal" that left the inadvertent scorer, Christian Zaccardo, looking shell-shocked with dismay.

But if anyone expected Zaccardo's teammates to shun him for his error, they were mistaken. This Italian team had more camaraderie than any in recent soccer history, and it showed in every game they played. While there were standouts, to be sure, those players never put individual achievements ahead of their main goal — namely, winning the championship.

"If we really play as a team, as we know we can," Alessandro Del Piero commented in the days before the match, "then we can win."

Anchored by their goalkeeper Gianluigi Buffon, the Italians were one of the most balanced of any team in the tournament. With equal parts defensive might, outstanding midfield coverage, and offensive power, Italy boasted a combination that looked ripe for victory.

Of course, the French had their strengths, too, which led them to the final round. Chief among those strengths was their superstar, Zinedine Zidane, who at the age of thirty-three gave energetic perfor-mances game after game.

The two teams met in the historic Olympiastadion in Berlin for the finals. Nearly seventy thousand spec-tators filled the stands; millions in countries around the world tuned in at all hours to watch live coverage of the match.

The French struck first with a thunderous penalty kick by Zidane. The Italians answered soon after-ward with a header by Marco Materazzi on a corner kick. That's where the score stayed as minute after minute ticked by. Zidane nearly got France up by one with a header of his own. But just before the ball sailed under the crossbar, goalkeeper Gianluigi Buf-fon tipped it up and out with his fingertips.

Had Zidane's header gone in, it would have been the talk of the tournament. Instead, it was a different header by the Frenchman that had tongues wagging.

The score stayed knotted until the end of the sec-ond half, forcing the game into extra time. Twenty minutes into that time, Zidane made a move on Mat-erazzi. But the move wasn't aimed at the ball—it was a headbutt aimed at Materazzi himself!

What exactly happened before Zidane drilled his shaven head into Materazzi's chest? Film shows that the two were walking down the field side by side, apparently exchanging words. Materazzi seemed to tug at Zidane's shirt. Then Zidane quickened his pace and got ahead of Materazzi. Suddenly, he spun about and—*wham!*—slammed Materazzi with a massive headbutt.

Materazzi fell like a ton of bricks. The referee ran over, whipped out a red card, and waved it over Zidane. Zidane was ejected!

In later interviews, Zidane claimed that Materazzi had been insulting members of his family and that's why he attacked him. Materazzi himself has remained silent on the incident.

The game resumed minus Zidane. Neither team managed to score before the time ended. As in 1994, the match would be decided by a best-of-five penalty shoot-out.

Italy took the first kick. It was good. So was France's first attempt. Italy made their second as well. On France's next kick, disaster struck. Goalkeeper Buffon stared at David Trezeguet. Trezeguet took three steps and kicked. Buffon hurled himself toward the lower left corner of the net—but the ball flew high and to the right, a sure goal!

Except it wasn't. Incredibly, the ball struck the crossbar and cannoned straight down, just outside the line. No good!

If the Italians could make the rest of their shots, they would be the winners of World Cup 2006.

That's just what happened. When Fabio Grosso blasted the final kick past goalkeeper Fabien Barthez's reaching hands, the Italian players went insane with joy. "I knew if we scored our first penalty, we could score them all," Italian coach Marcello Lippi said, rejoicing.

And with them all, the Italians were once again world champions!

★ CHAPTER NINETEEN ★

1991, 1995, 1999, 2003, 2007

The Women's World Cup

It's one of the most enduring images in all of World Cup history. The player who had just blasted in the winning shot in the World Cup final's penalty shoot-out fell to her knees and whipped off her jersey.

That's right: *her* knees, *her* jersey. For the player was a woman named Brandi Chastain. In 1999, she and the rest of Team U.S.A. became soccer heroes.

The history of the FIFA's Women's World Cup is much shorter than that of the Men's. It began with Dr. João Havelange, FIFA's president, who recognized that soccer had become as popular with girls and women as it was with boys and men. Following in Jules Rimet's footsteps, he decided to do all he could to boost that popularity even higher. What better way than to create the female equivalent of the most popular sporting event in the world?

Like the first Men's World Cup, the first Women's World Cup was a modest affair with just twelve nations competing. Held in China in November of

1991, the stars of the tournament were from the United States: Carin Jennings, April Heinrichs, and Michelle Akers, known collectively as the "Triple-Edged Sword" for their scoring prowess. This trio was responsible for twenty of the teams twenty-five goals; Akers alone scored ten, including a five-goal effort in the win over Chinese Taipei.

While that performance was amazing, Akers's most significant goal came in the final match against Norway. The score was tied, 1–1, with just three minutes remaining in the game. Norway had control of the ball in front of their goal—or so it seemed until Tina Svensson passed back to goalie Reidun Seth.

The pass was bad. Akers swept in, captured the ball, dodged around Seth, and booted a shot into the unguarded net! The United States was up, 2–1! And when the clock ticked down minutes later, the American women had done what their male counterparts had never even come close to doing—they had won the World Cup.

The inaugural Women's Cup had been small in scale but a huge success overall. The second tournament, held in Sweden in 1995, was even better. It had an added bonus, doubling as the qualifier for the first women's Olympic football (soccer) tournament to be held the following year.

With the world championship and entrance to the

Olympics on the line, competition was fiercer than ever before. The United States was the heavy favorite, but when Akers was injured in the first match, some wondered if the team could pull off a repeat of its first triumph.

The Americans got one step closer to their goal in game two, an interesting match that found superstar forward Mia Hamm in a new position — goalkeeper! She took over the slot when Briana Scurry was ejected. Luckily, she played her part well enough to help the United States beat Denmark, 2–0.

The U.S. defeated the Australians in the next game, 4–1, and then put aside the Japanese team in the quarterfinals to reach the semifinals. That was as far as the Americans got, however. They lost to the Norwegian team, 1–0, and ended the tournament in third place overall.

The United States was the host country for the 1999 Women's World Cup. This tournament would be, in the words of FIFA, "the beginning of a new era of success for women's football . . . a milestone in the history of women's sports."

The competition was held in jam-packed stadiums throughout the United States. Many of the fans were young girls there to worship their heroes. Mia Hamm, Michelle Akers, Tiffeny Milbrett, Kristine Lilly, Joy Fawcett, and the rest were the epitome of the game's athleticism, competitive spirit, and grace in motion. But it wasn't just girls who hung on the team's every move.

"The whole country is caught up," then president Bill Clinton commented. And it was true. For three weeks that summer, women's soccer was the talk of the nation.

The Women's World Cup had grown from twelve to sixteen entrants. One by one, the United States knocked aside each team it faced to reach the final round. A few games were close, but most were decisive wins, and one was an absolute blowout that saw the United States pushing in five goals (six, counting an "own goal" by Nigeria) in one half alone.

But the United States was not the only team to go undefeated in the first rounds. The Chinese were just as dominant. In the semifinals, they blasted Norway out of the water, 5–0.

The Cup's final match, played in the Rose Bowl in Los Angeles, was one of the most watched sporting events in history. More than ninety thousand people crammed into the stands. Millions in the United States and elsewhere in the world tuned in to watch on television. All were witness to a match unparalleled in soccer history.

Forty-five minutes passed without a score. So did the next forty-five, which ended with the backbone of the American squad, Michelle Akers, being carried off on a stretcher. She had collided with Scurry on a Chinese corner kick. The impact was hard enough to send her to the ground. Doctors soon discovered that she was also dehydrated. The combination of conditions made Akers, as she said later, "loony."

With Akers gone, the Chinese almost took the win. But Lilly, backing Scurry up just inside the goal, stole their near victory by heading Fan Yunjie's header out of the danger zone.

"Just doing my job," Lilly commented.

The rest of the team members continued to do their jobs in the remaining time. But so did the Chinese defenders. At the end of a long thirty minutes, the score was still 0–0. The match would be decided by a best-of-five penalty shoot-out.

The Americans kicked first. Four players later, the teams were tied with two penalty goals apiece. Then Kristine Lilly drained hers to make it 3–2. Liu Ying readied herself for the third Chinese attempt.

As she did, goalkeeper Scurry noticed something. "Her shoulders were slumped, and she looked tired. I thought, this is the one." Sure enough, Scurry blocked Liu's shot, no problem.

Mia Hamm was up next. After two scoreless games, she had lost confidence in her shot. She got it back in the next instant when she powered a blast past the Chinese goalkeeper.

But the fifth and final Chinese kicker made her shot, too. The goal tally was now at four apiece. A win for the United States came down to one player, Brandi Chastain.

Chastain placed the ball on the line and stepped back. After a brief pause, she trotted forward and, with her left foot, booted the kick that went into the net — and made history.

"I thought, my God, this is the greatest moment of my life on the soccer field," a teary but joyful Chastain told reporters later.

It was a moment that would not be repeated in the future Women's World Cups. In 2003, the competition returned to the United States unexpectedly because of the SARS epidemic unfolding in China. On their home turf, the reigning champions were unseated in the semifinals by Germany, the eventual victors. The Germans successfully defended their title four years later in China with an exciting 2–1 win over Brazil.

It will be Germany again in 2011, at least as the new hosts of the Women's World Cup. How will the United States, third-place holders for the previous Cups, fare? How will the men do when they play in 2010, for that matter?

Only time — and talent — will tell. But a few things at least are certain: The competitions will be fierce. The action will be thrilling. New heroes will be born while once-shining stars will dim. Unexpected upsets will delight soccer-crazed nations and doom others to disappointment.

But no matter what happens, four years later and for generations to come, those same nations will have other chances at the ultimate soccer goal: the World Cup.

Men's FIFA World Cup Results

Year	Winner	Score	2nd Place	Host Country
1930	Uruguay	4–2	Argentina	Uruguay
1934	Italy	2–1 (aet)	Czechoslovakia	Italy
1938	Italy	4–2	Hungary	France
1950	Uruguay	2–1*	Brazil	Brazil
1954	West Germany	3–2	Hungary	Switzerland
1958	Brazil	5–2	Sweden	Sweden
1962	Brazil	3–1	Czechoslovakia	Chile
1966	England	4–2 (aet)	West Germany	England
1970	Brazil	4–1	Italy	Mexico
1974	West Germany	2–1	Netherlands	West Germany
1978	Argentina	3–1 (aet)	Netherlands	Argentina
1982	Italy	3–1	West Germany	Spain
1986	Argentina	3–2	West Germany	Mexico
1990	West Germany	1–0	Argentina	Italy
1994	Brazil	0–0 (3–2 PSO)	Italy	United States
1998	France	3–0	Brazil	France
2002	Brazil	2–0	Germany	Japan/South Korea
2006	Italy	1–1 (5–3 PSO)	France	Germany

*Score of decisive match of round-robin final round

Women's FIFA World Cup Results

Year	Winner	Score	2nd Place	Host Country
1991	United States	2–1	Norway	China
1995	Norway	2–0	Germany	Sweden
1999	United States	0–0 (5–4 PSO)	China	United States
2003	Germany	2–1 (aet)	Sweden	United States
2007	Germany	2–1	Brazil	China

aet = after extra time

PSO = Penalty Shootout

Read them all!

*Previously published as Crackerjack Halfback

All available in paperback from Little, Brown and Company

**Previously published as Pressure Play

***Previously published as Baseball Pals

Matt Christopher®

Muhammad Ali

Lance Armstrong

Kobe Bryant

Jennifer Capriati

Dale Earnhardt Sr.

Jeff Gordon

Ken Griffey Jr.

Mia Hamm

Tony Hawk

Ichiro

LeBron James

Derek Jeter

Randy Johnson

Michael Jordan

Peyton and Eli Manning

Yao Ming

Shaquille O'Neal

Albert Pujols

Jackie Robinson

Alex Rodriguez

Babe Ruth

Curt Schilling

Sammy Sosa

Tiger Woods